GENTLEMEN, START *HER* ENGINE

—AND KEEP IT RUNNING

350 Easy Ways to Forever Supercharge Your Lady's Heart

STEVEN A. GUERRERO

Quo Vadis

Diamond Bar, California

Cover art by Lainie Siege; design by Cathy Bowman.

First printing 2004

ISBN 0-9729946-4-5
LCCN 2003092025

ATTENTION CORPORATIONS, UNIVERSITIES, COLLEGES, AND PROFESSIONAL ORGANIZATIONS: Quantity discounts are available on bulk purchases of this book for educational, gift purposes, or as premiums for increasing magazine subscriptions or renewals. Special books or book excerpts can also be created to fit specific needs. For information, please contact Quo Vadis Books, 324 South Diamond Bar Boulevard, PMB 350, Diamond Bar, CA 91765; (909) 396-0383; sales@quovadisbooks.com; www.StartHerHeart.com.

"*If my words truly offer love's wisdom—*
Pure nutriment—let them be considered
Unto the hearts upon which Man feeds.
May he nourish them daily with love,
So selfish, his prayers needn't be."

—Steven A. Guerrero

CONTENTS

PART I: TEST-DRIVE THE COURSE

PART II: THE WORKBOOK—

Her Fuel Tank: 350 Ways to Forever Supercharge Your Lady's Heart

ACKNOWLEDGMENTS

There are three types of people in my life for whom I'll always be grateful. These people are responsible for encouraging me, motivating me, and inspiring me.

I want to thank everyone who in one way or another encouraged me to write this book. Those who encouraged me include every person who has ever asked me the question, "When are you going to write a book for men!?" or told me, "You need to write a book for men!" It also includes every person who has cooperated and helped make possible the unforgettable, outrageously romantic events or occasions I've arranged for my wife Angelica over the years; and they are:

Robert Lia, Executive Chef at Geoffrey's in Malibu, California; Ed Skolak and Pete Chiarenza of the Blue Dolphin Inn, Santa Barbara, California (sorry about the Jacuzzi tub, guys); the staff at Spanish Villa in Napa Valley, California; Darlyne Miller Kozi and Freemark Abbey Wines in Saint Helena, California (it's a dirty job, but…sorry about your chest, Darlyne); Amery Burleigh and service staff at the Four Seasons Biltmore Hotel and Restaurant in Santa Barbara, California (for the menu and much more); the service staff at George's at the Cove in La Jolla, California (for the free saucer and wearing the watch); Dr. Maureen Burney, Ph.D., (for believing in me); Bridgette Cheeks (massaging it, messaging it, it's all good); my good friend and phenomenal flamenco guitarist Anthony Arizaga (he does it his way); my dear friend Clifford Dejong (you make it happen, buddy).

My loving parents, married 40 years (and still they aren't sure if I'm of the same bloodline); my sister Cindy, brother-in-law Rudy,

Robert, Monica, Devana, Beatrice V. Grossman, Ricardo Calvero and family, Dorothy (Dottie) Sterris, Horatio Costa, Michael Walsh, Lainie Siegel, Gregory J.P Godek, Marilyn & Tom Ross, Cathy Bowman, Sue Collier, Lurina Thieman, Kate Deubert, Deb Ellis, Jennifer Quintana, Aunt Diane Joutigue, Jeff and Christy Lopez, Marie Holmes, Diane Tobar, Maria Jiron, Rich and Debbie Migala, Richard Rodriguez, Christine McGurty, Jean Jenkin, James Vita, Valerie A. Caires at UCLA (what a difference, huh, Valerie?), the late great Ralph Worthington (I read many beautiful things, but the wisdom of heart was what I found in your very own Garden of Eden, and I thank you) of course, I also thank each and every one of my family members and friends who have supported me along the way.

Now, to all of you who motivated me to continue. No matter what you thought or how tactless, arrogant, harsh, and truthful your opinions were sometimes, thank you for keeping the fire under my bum burning brightly. In our lives we learn most from those not easily influenced by consideration at a time when the truth is absolute. It's the stern teacher who eventually smiles at you that instills the most valuable and memorable lessons in life. However, there are some (and you know who you are) who failed to smile. But uncouth as they might seem, they do have a lesson to teach. Their delivery was far from kind, yet rich and constructive. In taking heed, smiles or no smiles, from you all I've learned loads—and for that I'm very thankful. Maybe the next time we meet it can be over a smile.

There are only two people in the world who inspired me to do this book. They are my lovely wife, best friend, and partner in life Angelica, and my brave little hero and superstar daughter Jessica. The two of you are the only ones to fulfill all three—encouraged, motivated, and inspired me—and you continue doing so. Not only have you made it possible for me to write this book, but you continue to make it easy for me to stay the man, who through love brings out the best in you both. I love you dearly.

INTRODUCTION

It's been said by many a wise individual that man often is the aggressor and initiates action. When you love your wife, what will she do? She will love you in return. If you are gentle and kind, she can respond to you in similar fashion. However, if you are inconsiderate, sarcastic, and brutal, she can strike back with rebellion. The man is to be the giver. The woman is to respond to what she receives. Even our bodies have been designed in such a way physically that the woman receives the man.

Gentlemen, in case you haven't heard, more than two thirds of divorces are initiated by women. Then we have the 60 percent of married men who have admitted to cheating on their wives and the 40 percent of married women who have admitted to cheating on their husbands. It's ugly. So I'm sure you'll agree we need to do something to decrease—if not entirely abolish—those (nasty) numbers.

Among the leading factors contributing to our society's horrific marital statistics are those linked directly to the lack of, and in many cases complete absence of, the man's willingness to be thoughtful, helpful, appreciative, and romantic toward his mate. A man's reluctance to improve and perform in the above-mentioned areas of a relationship has also been proven to cause a woman to feel as though she is no longer loved and appreciated by him; consequently, she grows apart from him.

Caution! Research studies show that "not feeling loved and appreciated" and "growing apart from him" continue to rank as the top two reasons women file for divorce. Money, infidelity, and domestic, alcohol or drug-related abuse are no longer even found among the five leading reasons women choose to file for the big "D." This doesn't make it okay for men everywhere to run out and quit their job, get a mistress, and join the reefer referendum. It is merely to point out the most beneficial areas men should be concerned about improving the most.

What can you do to avoid becoming this frightening trend's next victim wherein your woman leaves you for difficulties you have yet to find a solution for? Or how do you, having never been taught, all of a sudden learn the things you can do so the thought of leaving you never enters your honey's mind?

I've discovered a long overlooked simple solution and targeted plan of action that is sure to help men avoid getting divorced for the two most common reasons these days. My discoveries will help men reduce if not entirely eliminate the possibility of their partner's choosing to drop out of the "relationship race" for good. I'm excited to be sharing this valuable information with you in the upcoming chapters.

When my solution is combined with the proper plan of action, it quickly amounts to helping men discover easier ways to avoid the most common cause of women divorcing them—which until now has remained as confusing as a European race car engine to a moped mechanic. But not anymore. Now it can be easy for a man to always please the woman he loves. Here is the basis of my solution: Gentlemen, you need to always keep in mind the top two reasons women continue to file for divorce, which I believe are not likely to change. It's the same as avoiding lung cancer. If you don't want to die an ugly premature death, don't start smoking cigarettes—or try very hard to quit.

Now for those of you men who prefer the woman you love never leaves you: When you've embedded into your memory bank the two main reasons women choose to divorce, above, then you'll have the mind-set to continue to use the materials in this book to create and follow a successful plan of action.

Now imagine yourself being a race car driver. This book and the workbook are the highly trained auto mechanics and pit crew on your team. Think of the relationship between you and your significant other as the "relationship race." The mechanics and pit crew members must be properly trained and certified before they can even be considered for the job. By having the right specialists on your crew, you will have a team of experts whose impeccable knowledge of the automobile will help keep it running at its peak performance, ensuring lap after exhilarating lap around the track. But, if you hire just anyone, or even worse no one at all, your car may not perform to the desired level and may leave you broken down and stranded.

Just like the race car, your woman also has many different areas you should properly maintain, service, and upgrade on a regular basis. By gathering and documenting the right information about her, it can benefit your relationship in ways similar to that of how a race car and its driver benefit from having a team of expert mechanics and pit crew. The information you'll be documenting in Part II of this book can help keep you and your sweetheart running perfectly, in tune with one another in the "relationship race."

Whether you're reading this book because of negligence or you just want to nurture and improve your relationship, you have revealed a desire to make a change for the better. You've made a choice to improve your life and the life of the woman you love and respect. And she deserves it.

The *Gentlemen, Start Her Engine* book and workbook are overflowing with simple, powerful, and permanent ways to become more romantic, knowledgeable, thoughtful, and helpful when it comes to caring for the lady in your life. She'll begin to recognize your attempts as your appreciation of her, as well as a romantic aphrodisiac whose potency can surely impress you. Not only will you find she's becoming more understanding and cooperative toward your needs (not just of the sexual kind either), but you can forget about ever having a guilty conscience while indulging in and enjoying many of your own favorite things—in moderation of course.

Part I of the book is your training course, designed to familiarize you with the basic requirements that will not only help you qualify for the "relationship race" but keep you returning to victory lane. When you're done with Part I, you'll have discovered hundreds of easy things you can do to assure your sweetheart always feels loved and appreciated by you. The lady in your life can only feel like the two of you are growing together as one.

Part II of the book is titled "Her Fuel Tank: 350 Ways to Forever Supercharge Your Lady's Heart." This workbook section has been referred to by Marilyn Ross as, and I quote, "a priceless treasure in itself, it makes it so *easy* for a man to be romantic, consistently attentive, and totally tuned into his woman!" I'll bet that makes you want to start at the back of the book. In truth, a man could improve his relationship and benefit tremendously by simply completing and using the workbook section. However, his rewards and benefits will never be as great as those of the men who consume every page of this book from beginning to end.

Once you've finished reading Part I, you'll really know how to use and benefit from Part II. Your completion of the workbook section can be quick, fun, and simple. All the information I've designed for you to collect in the workbook is already categorized and in list format for convenience. What you're going to learn and discover about the woman in your life is nothing short of powerful. When your workbook is completed, you'll have in your possession, access to "350 Ways to Forever Supercharge Your Lady's Heart." And that's *not* including the ideas you get in Part I.

One other thing before I turn you loose: If you're a father or ever plan on being one, think about this for a minute. Most daughters grow up loving and respecting their daddies very much. The watchful eyes of a little girl are focused on her daddy much of the time—and his behavior toward her mommy. The day will come when daddy's little girl is all grown up, a young woman looking for a companion. Studies have shown that many women choose men who are like their fathers. So, if the example a daddy sets as a husband is loving, affectionate, helpful, and domesticated, these oftentimes can be just a few of the good qualities his daughter will seek in a mate. Now imagine if the qualities above were disrespectful, inconsiderate, selfish, chauvinistic, abusive. Need I say more?

Let's not forget about the boys. If you're raising a son or eventually want to, consider this: All too often the misconceptions a boy learns about the role of a wife and mother are taught to him by his father. Add to that his father's impotent examples of the love, respect, and gratitude for his wife and a father has paved love's road to failure for his son. Your son can end up miserably married and maybe divorced. Thinking the grass is greener on the other side of the fence, he will roll in it feverishly. But this temporary happiness will fill his landscape until, again by his own doing, the greener pasture withers and dies.

Now more than ever, gentlemen, we should be looking to do whatever it takes to increase not only our own odds but those for our children to remain not just married but *happily* married. To achieve this goal, we must be powerful and positive role models for our children. So, carefully evaluate what you've learned from your father, grandfather, and great-grandfather about women and how to care for them properly.

Chances are if your mother was the happiest woman in the world because of how your father treated her, she would tell you joyfully. You would have also witnessed their beautiful love story firsthand and center stage while growing up. But for a lot of men, their mothers never exhibited signs of being unhappily married—at least not in front of them. Therefore, it's more than likely a very large number of the male population still believe if their mother was happy with the way their father treated her, their partners should be happy with the same. It's the big fat misconception that continues to plague man's ability to make a woman happy for a lifetime.

Beyond this page lies the truths to many of the questions left unanswered that pertain to women and how we can keep them happy today and well into the future. So strap yourself in, keep your eyes on the road, and I'll see you in victory lane.

Part I

TEST-DRIVE
THE COURSE

CHAPTER I

THE RELATIONSHIP INFORMATION RACE

How You Could Be Choosing to Win or Lose

We are living in the information age, and it seems we can't stop compiling it, searching for more of it, and storing the likes of it. New high-tech tools are developed almost daily to improve efficiency for the accessing, collecting, managing, and mobility of our increasing need to capture and store information. The tools developed seem to accommodate society's everyday need to get organized and be available in almost every imaginable way known to humankind. First there was the home computer with its database management tools. Then the laptop made us portable. Arriving next was the personal digital assistant, or PDA, basically a handheld computer. Today we are wireless on the web and taking snapshots and videos with our cell phones and, not to mention sending and receiving e-mail with them. And it's just the beginning.

Technology has been updated, but we've overlooked something else that is in dire need of improvement and updating: interaction with women. How to make them happy and keep them happy.

By collecting, researching, documenting, and storing pertinent information, businesses dramatically increase their chance of survival. Without profound knowledge of the industry they're in, difficulty or failure may be the result. When it comes to loving a woman, the same value and benefit created by possessing quality information, as in the previous business example, applies to the man who wants to succeed in keeping his woman happy forever. The type of important information a man will benefit to collect and know about his honey includes a rather large variety of specific items and categories. I have included all of the particulars a woman could love, want, and need her man to know. I can guarantee an improvement in your relationship, but only if you follow my instruction. To educate yourself with the information this book has to offer you about your partner can only help you to keep your relationship dynamic— as it was in the beginning.

It seems as though we have yet to apply any type of method for gathering and permanently storing important information pertaining to our mates. Although the fear of failing could be what keeps many of us from trying to improve, one of our most notorious adversaries is accountability. Accountability demands results. It also requires taking action, and judgment awaits those who don't. Scary, isn't it? To think we might have to keep on doing nice things in order to keep our honey happy, forever. The only thing scarier is what happens after we stop making an effort.

If a man occasionally studied the things he has taken the time to learn about his partner's needs and desires—made aware of their importance in relation to her happiness—his responsibility to please her would become undeniably feasible. The more a man knows about his woman's needs and desires, the more accountable he becomes. Especially when he possesses as much knowledge as is in this book. Any excuse he makes thereafter (despite how creative) for not trying to fulfill the needs and desires of his sweetheart could merely be interpreted as lack of interest and appreciation of her. That's the epitome of an insult to any woman and will eventually spawn the deterioration of trust in her man.

Whether it's improving your relationship with your beloved, losing or controlling your weight, excelling in the workplace, paying bills on time, saving for retirement, or achieving any goal—remaining 100 percent accountable is essential. Most individuals who exhaust little effort or slack off in the few areas mentioned above tend to experience minor but mostly major difficulties during their lifetime. Slackers almost always reap much less than they expect and often wonder why. Could you be slacking off just a bit in your relationship? Maybe you've even reached your full slack-off potential in one or more areas of your life. Don't feel bad. I know what it's like. I was once a slacker myself—the portly type.

On that note I'd like to share briefly with you a true story of my own battle with accountability. At the same time I'll point out to you how the combination of correctly used and properly gathered information made it extremely easy for me to remain accountable and therefore succeed.

Accountability 240

At one time in my life, I was lugging around 240 pounds. (Back then I still thought of it as semi-solid muscle.) But at only 5 feet 10 inches tall, the only solid thing left on my body was my head. I continued to deny the truth. I was finally scared out of my 40-inch waist jeans by an episode of angina pectoris. For those of you who aren't familiar with the term "angina pectoris," it's a reaction of the human body that can make you feel like you're about to have a heart attack—and practically scared me into having one. That's when I finally awoke to see in the mirror the reflection of a fat guy with fat arms.

Wearing my baggiest T-shirt and elastic waistband shorts, I hit the gym embarrassed and scared. My fear was that I'd run into somebody I went to high school with, who was now buff and with a full head of hair. But even worse, I might be reunited with a tanned, in-shape woman who once had a crush on me in school.

But not even the fear of humiliation could keep me from restoring my health. About a week after I started working out again and eating less, I bumped into an old friend of mine named Eric. Eric had become a licensed fitness trainer and bodybuilder. And was he ever in great shape. Lean and buff, he was doing everything right. Unfortunately he didn't have the same to say about me. After 45 dollars and several weeks of regular trips to the gym, I lost 30 pounds and was sporting a 30-inch waist. The strange thing was, I was eating more food than before. But it was the right food.

I was feeling like a high school senior all over again. My mission had been accomplished. But by no means did the money I paid to Eric buy me some miracle diarrhea diet, fat loss drug, or trapper enzymes in a bottle. No. What my weekly fast-food fund bought me was a tailor-made menu (gathered information). The menu had a variety of healthy tasty foods in the right sized portions—making it easy for me to stay accountable. The portions were determined by my age, weight, and overall physical condition (more targeted gathered information). The program was tailor-made for me and no one else. Along with the menu there was a thorough workout program (also gathered information), which included detailed weight training and cardiovascular exercise routines.

Only by following Eric's advice and programs was I able to achieve the results I wanted. I can never thank Eric enough for sharing his priceless knowledge with me, then guiding me in the right direction. His targeted program made it easy for me to be successful by remaining accountable.

The content and application of this book are designed to do the same thing Eric and his program did for me: guarantee results. The only difference is in the type of results. I know you're not reading this book to learn how to lose weight and keep it off. But I'll bet you're interested in finding ways to keep from ever losing the lady you love. You'll be learning how to follow my targeted methods, similar to my custom menu , only this time it pertains to many of your sweetheart's needs and desires. When you've finished the workbook, you'll know all the right things to do for your honey and by sticking to them you can continue to keep her, yourself, and the relationship emotionally healthy, strong, and on the racetrack of happiness.

In certain cases, immediate results can elude even the most noteworthy of men. When your desire is to make your honey happy, not only does it require patience, but courage as well if you're to continue to keep her happy. We should always give freely, especially to our loved ones. If you stick to the program, you'll eventually begin to produce a positive "snowball effect" in your relationship. The results will be well worth the wait, which most of the time isn't long.

How many of you don't balance your checkbook? How about your taxes, do you keep track of them? Do you have a budget? What about the annual business plan? Nevertheless, plenty of us get by and go through our life in a semi-peaceful fashion, even though we procrastinate and manage the above tasks poorly . But to say the least, you and I and everyone else have got to have a little black book, daily planner, or PDA. Whichever you have, at the least it's probably loaded with the names, addresses, and telephone numbers of immediate family members and dear friends. Right?

What's the worst thing that can happen without doing and maintaining any of the above-mentioned items? That's right. We could go broke, get audited, and possibly be disowned by our family or friends. Being broke, getting audited, or losing a family member or a dear friend can all be difficult to cope with even when your relationship is a happy, healthy one. But whenever you experience trying times like those I just mentioned, while in a miserable marriage or relationship, they can become unbearable and sometimes be the last straw in the cocktail of love.

Are you thinking this sounds like too much work—and unnecessary? Do you believe if something doesn't come natural, then it shouldn't be required? Well, the truth is, there's always gonna be those guys whose ball bill for a round of golf exceeds the cost of their green fees with a cart—despite their 20-some years of Sundays out on the links. True, every man reserves the right to remain crappy at something. Golf is one respectable choice. But choosing not to care about what kind of husband and father we are, and the example we set in our homes...well, come on, men, let's show some dignity here.

Take a serious look at the areas in your life where you devote most of your time and energy toward improving. Are those areas related to everything but the relationship with your mate? If your answer is "yes" or "I'm a 6 handicap" and you're not on the PGA tour, you might want to consider changing the order of your priorities. I'm not saying give up your hobbies, but you could benefit greatly by improving the most important areas of life first—spirituality, marriage, family, and health. Seek a better balance. Complete the workbook section of this book and an evaluation of your relation-

GENTLEMEN, START *HER* ENGINE—And Keep It Running

ship with your partner will be in the palm of your hand; don't ever let it go.

I always thought natural was meant for things like gas, giving birth, and receding hairlines.

If you have a habit of using unnaturalness as an excuse to be selfish or lazy, watch out. Eventually your deliberate diversions can result in your having to accept accountability in its worst light. Your woman just may withdraw from you and seek out someone who is more in touch with nature. Whose accountability will it be then?

We men are capable of doing anything we set our mind to—far more than we have led the women in our lives to believe.

Take sports, for example. A woman once told me, she knows this man—her husband—who can remember the height, weight, biceps measurement, and season statistics of many professional athletes and teams. Unfortunately, he can't remember what his wife's favorite color is or much else related to her. A lot of men possess vast amounts of knowledge in the area of sports trivia, which tragically seems to far exceed what they know about the women they love.

All of this talk about how to please a woman reminds me of a research study I once read about in a best-selling book about relationships. The study found that when men feel needed by their partner, they become motivated to fulfill her needs for love, romance, and support.

So, why do so many women still complain about men being selfish, boring, inconsiderate of their feelings, needs, and desires, and not romantic enough? I'll tell you why. It's because there are so many things—romantic and not romantic—men need to know about the woman they love if they want to continue to make her happy. But there is only one way for men to discover those things: *Ask!* And there is only one way to ensure we never forget them: *Write them down!* By doing those two things you gain an enormous increase in knowledge about your loved one and improve your abilities to do the things she loves, tenfold. I will help get you to that stage of the race.

I'll be the first to admit that most men need instructions—especially in this area. The Gentlemen, Start *Her* Engine concept provides

14

you with timeless solutions, a practical plan of action, and easy-to-use everyday tools. As for the instructions—you're already reading them.

Sure it's a good idea to know the reasons people can feel the way they feel. To know why people do the things they do isn't such a bad idea either. But what do you do then? From that point forward it's critical you are guided in the proper direction. I suggest equipping you with tools to locate and keep track of your partner's specific needs and desires. Then I'll keep you in the lead by giving you numerous ideas for how to use your information to create consistent, easy-to-do good deeds, sure to keep her heart's RPM strong.

To have lists, like those in the workbook, filled with information specifically related to your sweetheart—things she likes, dislikes, needs, and desires—enables you to possess a thorough understanding of her. The lists in the workbook offer you a permanent source to access whenever you choose (or need) to provide anything for your significant other. Gift ideas, romantic gestures, affection, emotional support, all the do's and don'ts about your honey you can find and more, in your workbook.

As this same study also discovered, women are motivated and empowered to please when they feel cherished. Until this book, nobody has shown men how to determine and do things that make their own woman feel cherished. Now that's what I call profound. Gentlemen, I'm beginning to believe when it comes to women, many of us were taught 2 + 2 = 5. But don't be discouraged, because my equation adds up correctly: using this book = a woman who constantly feels cherished and therefore is motivated and empowered to please her man.

I'm confident once you begin to see the results in comparison to the amount of time required to produce them, not only will you be pleased by the overwhelming joy of your mate, but you'll be convinced by the rewarding relationship you've begun to experience with her. I think enough has been said to encourage you to give the suggestions I'll be sharing with you a try. If you already have a wonderful relationship, great, you can only improve upon it. But if you're experiencing an unsatisfying relationship, you have nothing to lose and everything to gain by trying something new. For those of you not yet involved with anyone, this book can still help you tremendously. When you find that special woman, you'll know what you can expect and how to keep her devoted to you. You will be able to offer her a lifetime of love and happiness to cherish forever.

"To find the woman of your dreams and possibly even create her—first be the man of hers. If your wish is to keep her as a dream, stay one yourself."

—Steven A. Guerrero

CHAPTER 2

FROM "BABY WALKERS" TO "BIG BLOCKS"

A Quick Drive Through Memory Lane

Most of us are unable to remember anything from our infancy. Why is that? Certainly, it must be because infants lack the ability to interpret words. However, constantly being touched, held, hugged, kissed, smiled at, and fed are just a few of the things that keep those little buggers so happy. And so it is with properly nurtured infants that they learn to recognize and appreciate love, first, through actions not words.

When we reach a certain age, we begin to develop a mediocre comprehension of words. Many of us had parents who often failed to acknowledge their feelings toward us by saying, "I love you." When parents did verbally express their love, it was frequently followed by some authenticating speech. We were informed of how physical evidence should be seen and interpreted as their love for us. Many times the speeches consisted of hovering phrases like, "Buy the roof over your head," "The clothes on your back," "See those shoes on your feet," "That food on the table," and, "Do you know why we go to work every day?" The lucky ones might have heard phrases like, "What about that bicycle you're riding," "Those little league seasons," "Those piano lessons you're taking," and many other luxuries. But all that we really wanted was to be read to or played with. Then

17

one day we came of age and were sent out into the real world, on our own. Before too long we would find ourselves struggling with social acceptance, trying to understand the opposite sex, and searching for a love that is blind.

Could the willingness to please our partner, be creative and help-ful, and continue to express love to them be due to our inability as infants to store the memories of and recall our most tender experi-ences with love and attentiveness? I believe it has a lot to do with it. Either you've come a long way to be reading a book like this or you have a ways to go until you recognize the importance of its contents. Everyone might agree that from birth, we appreciated those who took the time and made the effort to remember the things we en-joyed and needed most.

Have you ever heard about the studies of humans regarding when and why they sometimes assume the fetal position? Research has led many of us to believe that we felt the safest while residing in our mother's womb in the fetal position. For about nine months, we floated contentedly, unaware of the delivery and instant supernova status that awaited us. While studying individuals who are in the midst of a severe emotional crisis, researchers found that a subject's need to get into a fetal position seemed to be a subconscious attempt to return to a place where he or she felt secure and protected from the outside world—the womb.

However, I've yet to meet a man or woman who possesses any memories of a motorized spoon or their incredible love for the game of peek-a-boo. Nor have I come across anyone who can describe the decor inside their mother's womb. Yet somehow most of us equate love and security with our loving, caring mothers. This leads me to believe that many experts are putting far too much emphasis on ver-bal communication, when, in fact, from the very beginning of our lives we were conditioned by a completely different example of how to communicate love—through actions.

Don't get me wrong; I'm also in support of those individuals who emphasize necessity in solving a verbal communication mystery be-tween the sexes. If it works for you, great. But there are more than two planets in our solar system and no two stars are alike. We should invest more time and effort toward finding out more about our mate's needs and desires. It's critical for any man to be aware of and able to provide in the many different areas of his honey's life—emotional, physical, tangible, sentimental, and spiritual.

Why did your mother change your diaper? Aside from the obvious answer, the reason was because accepting responsibility is associated with love. Why did she take the time to remember the foods you enjoyed the most—nutritious and some not so nutritious? What about all the other things she remembered to do for you because they were your favorites or good for you emotionally? The answer to those questions is that love also has the desire to fulfill. Love makes sure that physical and emotional nourishment are provided in a way that is desirable whether or not it is always convenient. Love will go out of its way to please. Maybe your mother did force you to eat your spinach once in a while—it was good for you—but it probably wasn't on the menu every day.

From the moment we were born, our mothers (and fathers) more than likely paid much attention to us. Also, most moms and pops cared enough to learn and remember what their kiddies loved and needed most. Our parents would do their best to provide; this made us feel secure, special, and most of all loved. As a child, if you didn't experience that kind of love, or as an adult you simply have no recollection of it, either could be the cause of your inability or unwillingness to provide for your honey's special needs and desires. The way we're loved as a child, I believe, is how we should love the woman in our life. It's time we start learning how to do more and say less.

Throughout your reading, I'm sure you'll find many of my examples may not necessarily apply to your sweetheart. That's what this book and workbook are all about. They provide lists of nearly everything you could ever need to know in order to please *your* loved one.

To make it easier for you to continue finding accurate ways to please your lady, you're always welcome to visit my website at www.StartHerHeart.com. There you'll find free tips, ideas, and a whole lot more to rev up her Hemi. At my website there are a variety of relationship resources for you to access. It is the most unique and targeted site on the web pertaining to women and how to make them happy. Unlike any other website, my site is dedicated and designed to focus on the special needs and desires of three typical styles of women. Men will be able to easily determine which style they are involved with and how to treat them accordingly.

The website is designed to provide men with ideas that work best for their women. This way you don't waste time sorting through hundreds—even thousands—of tips and ideas that don't relate to your sweetheart or her unique circumstances.

I'll show you how to determine which engine style your woman is in Chapter 7. Even without the website, you'll still find this book loaded with plenty of great examples for what, when, where, how, and why that you can apply. When you have completed filling in your workbook, you'll be free to choose from and use anything you've learned your special someone adores and needs.

What you're about to read is the first of many examples for how you can use the information you collect about your sweetheart. All the examples and scenarios you will be reading are achievable and realistic. The reason I've used them in the book is because I've in fact done and continue to do almost all of them for my wife.

I admit that I'm a bit of an extremist when it comes to romance, creativity, and being attentive to a woman's needs. You may not need to do the same things to the same degree that I do but still achieve a phenomenal result.

The following list of items is an example of the type of information you will be able to document about your own sweetheart:

♥ Her favorite wine is Freemark Abbey Merlot.

♥ Her favorite foods to eat when she drinks wine are apples, grapes, strawberries, fresh sourdough bread, cheese, crackers, and anything chocolate for dessert.

♥ Her favorite romantic music is Spanish love songs. You turned her on to the Gipsy Kings; she has never been the same since.

♥ The city that she has always wanted to visit is Napa, California—the wine country.

♥ Her favorite flowers are red roses and she especially enjoys getting just one sometimes, for no occasion at all—just because.

♥ She loves candlelight and hot baths.

♥ Her favorite massage oil is from Glen Ivy Resort and Spa in Temecula, California.

♥ She loves to use bath oils and bubble baths.

♥ She loves sentimental things—keepsakes.

This wealth of knowledge is all documented by you and kept easily accessible in your workbook. When you're ready to begin planning something for her birthday, you use the information to help you create and arrange the most unforgettable surprise weekend she's ever experienced. Your plan is for the two of you to take a trip up north to the city she has always wanted to visit—Napa. So you make reservations at a romantic Spanish-style bed and breakfast you locate on the Internet. It just so happens the winery that produces her favorite wine is walking distance from where you'll be staying. So a couple weeks in advance, over the phone, you begin to make your special arrangements with the bed and breakfast manager. She accommodates your every request to help prepare the suite in which you will be staying. You fax her a detailed list of things to do prior to your arrival. The list includes your instructions on how she is to prepare the room before the two of you arrive. Via your credit card, your honey's favorite wine and flowers are ordered and scheduled to be delivered to the bed and breakfast manager on the morning of your arrival. Continuing to follow your instructions, an hour before your estimated arrival time the manager will place in your room the roses, two wine glasses, and the opened bottle of wine (breathing) just waiting to be poured.

Before leaving on your trip, you pack the following items in a cooler: fruits, bread, cheeses, crackers, and chocolates—all of which you have learned, from your workbook, are among her favorites to consume with wine. Then you place the cooler in the trunk of your car, where the birthday girl won't see.

Earlier that week you picked up a gift basket for her filled with her favorite bubble baths, massage oil, and facial masks from the resort spa she mentioned was her favorite. The basket is also hidden in the trunk of the car. Since the trunk is now off limits to her, you need to be completely and stealthily in charge of the loading of the luggage.

Don't shut the trunk just yet; there are still a few more items to be packed. There's a portable compact disc player, CDs of her favorite romantic music, and an arsenal of scented candles. But the gift of all gifts is the professionally framed poem you wrote just for her. Incorporated into the framing is a picture of the two of you kissing. Also mounted inside of the frame is the star jasmine flower (now dried) you picked for her outside a restaurant where you and she had your first romantic dinner together. The dried jasmine flower is glued to the center of one very sentimental coffee saucer with a heart-shaped coffee stain on it from that very night. (I had noticed the stain and asked to purchase the saucer but our server was romantic enough to let us have it. He got a nice fat tip.) All these items are a tribute to that unforgettable dinner occasion. Just a little thought went into the preparation of that gift. I always knew I'd have a use for that saucer one day.

As you previously arranged with the bed and breakfast manager, when you arrive, you give your birthday girl an extensive tour of the grounds around the back of the inn. During that time, the bed and breakfast manager was completing your instructions she received earlier that week. After locating the spare key you informed her would be in the ash tray of the car, she proceeded to remove all the items from the trunk of the car and place them strategically about the room. When you and your beloved entered the room, the candles are lit, her favorite music is playing, the gift basket, wine, flowers, and chocolates are all made visible to her. As for the poem, it is hanging on the wall where she eventually found it.

You couldn't believe the look on her face when she realized all that had been done. Her eyes filled with tears while she stood refusing to believe that anyone would go to all this trouble to please her.

The rest of the weekend was spent spoiling her with hot bubble baths, full body messages, and facial treatments. Years later she is still thanking you for a memory that will always be cherished and remains memorialized on the wall and entry table in the home where the two of you now live as a happily married couple.

Many men would not continue reading further if they thought it was expected of them to always organize events similar to the one you've just read. You're correct to notice the incredible amount of planning, motivation, and creative skills that can be required of a man who is to arrange events such as the previous one. Just in case you've forgotten, I will now ask you to please turn back to page 20 and again read the sentence that in all my anticipation of this very moment, I have marked in bold type to reiterate one of the most important things you can remember while reading this book.

The simple fact is, most, if not all women, would be enthralled if the man they love, cared to remember one of their favorite things more than just a few times a year. I've found that seldom do I have to go to extremes to continue having a profound impact on my wife. So it's not every day or even every month that I arrange something extravagant. With that in mind, seriously consider this: It's imperative you remember, as men, we are being measured more by our ability to be consistent and accurate with more precise, frequent gestures, which come in many different forms. When a man decides he is going to provide for a woman, through any kind of gesture, his ability to be accurate according to the woman's likings seems to be one of the keys to her long-term satisfaction in the relationship.

When you provide her only the things you know she loves and eliminate those things she doesn't care for, the message you'll send to her is that you must be very interested in her and her happiness to have learned so much about her. To a woman there probably aren't many other ways a man can express his love and appreciation for her that pack such a wallop.

Whether you aspire to create moments that will leave her breathless, or your goal is simply to become more consistent and accurate when providing for her needs, you have come to the right place to learn how to do both. But first we need to make sure that two out of the five human senses are properly tuned if you're planning to stay in this race. In many cases these two senses have been known to become idly useless to a man shortly after he secures the pole position, i.e., the best starting position in an auto race.

CHAPTER 3

KEEP YOUR EYES ON THE ROAD AND STEER WITH YOUR EARS

Two Human Senses Rebuilt Into Sensors

Of the five human senses—hearing, sight, touch, taste, and smell—to hear and see are the most essential to increase our awareness of other people, namely our loved ones. We're in dire need of enhancing the use of these two senses in particular. It will benefit you tremendously to know how and why to rebuild your sense of hearing and sight, converting them into "sensors" for recognizing valuable information pertaining to your partner. Especially if you desire to continue improving your relationship with her. First, let's look at how and why rebuilding your sense of hearing can help.

Rebuilding Your Sense of Hearing into a Sensor for Listening to Her Carefully.

Right now you're probably saying to yourself, "But I hear her loud and clear every day already." Well then, let me give you some sound (sound) advice. You wouldn't have to hear her so much if you knew how to listen to her carefully. Pay sharp attention to everything she says. The sooner you make friends with her words, the

25

sooner they can work for you rather than against you. And when you need them most—her words, that is—they'll be there for you. However, if you choose to have selective hearing, as many of us frequently do, you'll miss critical information.

I don't mean for you to be so attentive that you will no longer pull over for the paramedics, but here's one example of a great opportunity for you to be all ears.

Some call it quality time, or undivided attention. A dinner date is just one of many great times you can listen carefully to your honey. By listening to her closely during this time, you can find out a lot of new and useful information. You can learn about her favorite restaurants, menu items, drinks, ambiances, and music. If these bits of information sound trivial to you, just wait and see how I show you to use them to your advantage. All by itself this type of information can be used to make her feel like you know her like no other. Believe me, if there is one form of flattery a woman appreciates—more than any other—it would have to be a man's ability to communicate a great interest in her by his impeccable ability to provide her with the things she likes, needs, and wants, with rarely ever needing to ask her.

Once you're tuned into her, wherever the two of you might be, the second human sense known as sight becomes critical.

Rebuilding Your Sense of Sight into a "Sensor" for Watching Her Closely

Again let's use the dinner date as an example. During this time when you're already listening to her carefully, you want to engage your visual focus on her as well. Listening to and watching a woman simultaneously qualifies as the greatest combination since peanut butter and jelly. Always give your undivided attention to your sweetheart during quality time—not anyone or anything else around you. Use this time to notice how she responds to certain things. Your sense of sight is not only to see her but to watch her closely—like some of us watch the clock at work, study the green before we putt, and scream at anyone who walks in front of the television during our favorite sporting event.

26

Learn to look at her, or one day look at her leaving. Learn to watch her closely, or watch her eventually get close to someone else. Learn to pay close attention to her, or pay her alimony and child support. A history of relationship statistics proves it's only a matter of time before one of the above or worse can eventually occur from a man's careless behavior toward his mate.

Numerous benefits can, however, result from the proper use of our sense of hearing and sight at the appropriate times and places. One of the greatest benefits of your overhauling these two senses is the elimination of your lady thinking you've lost interest in her. Now, when you put your two cents (senses) in, it can produce an interest she's sure to recognize is in her favor. When the two of you are enjoying an intimate dinner date together or just a drink during a happy hour, be sure to always make eye contact with her when she's speaking to you.

While on a date of any kind, don't let yourself stare at televisions. Leave behind any newspapers, magazines, or work-related materials. Because when you make eye contact with someone, it's virtually impossible not to listen to what they're saying. And always avoid engaging in the second most popular, great American pastime: people watching. In our case, the people would be other women. I bet you already knew that.

Your sincere attempt to follow this advice and instruction will enable you to continue to learn new and useful information. When you complete the lists in the workbook, anything thereafter you discover about your sweetheart with your newly fine-tuned sensors will create more opportunities. When you give her your undivided attention at the proper times, she'll always feel secure about your interest in her.

Now here is an example of how our senses of hearing and sight did or didn't benefit some of us in the past. Think back for a minute to when you were in high school or college. Do you remember the effects on your performance in class if you failed to pay attention, collect pertinent information, and study? I'll bet you can recall difficulties and low marks being two effects out of many other undesirable ones from which to choose. In love relationships would you agree even fewer individuals pay attention to their sweethearts, collect pertinent information about them, and study them? Shamefully, in relationships today, more individuals adhere to a standard that is inferior to even the most lackadaisical standard some set in school. People are doing and giving just enough of themselves to squeak by in their relationships, and it's why so many are failing in love today and dropping out tomorrow.

Consequently, no matter how well we learned our subjects in school, the minute we stop using them they can quickly be forgotten. Right this minute if someone handed you a trigonometry test, history quiz, or any subject you hadn't seen the likes of for 10 or 20 years, would you be able to achieve a passing grade? Could you even complete the exam? When it comes to the subject of women, men need to continue to improve and remain committed to learning. Many men still refuse to adapt to the changed environment in their relationship and because of it eventually end up with a "D" (divorce) on their permanent record.

For those of you who may have occasionally cheated your way through school, I offer you this for consideration: History has shown some 60 percent of men have cheated on their wives. Is it any wonder women have trust issues? Meanwhile, some relationship experts still advise women to make an effort to fulfill a man in an area considered to be one of his primary love needs: trust. Hmm. If you were a woman, could you trust a man who put you on his list of priorities somewhere below watching *Sports Center* and right above getting a prostate examination? What will you do today, tomorrow, next week, next month, and for the rest of your commitment to your honey to assure her you're in the 40 percent of the men not searching for answers atop the sheets of another?!

When a woman recognizes you have a devoted interest in her, she can feel secure about your love for her—a definite precursor for trust. Once you've read the entire book and filled in your workbook section, opportunities to please your honey will present themselves left and right. It's entirely up to you, however, to take advantage of as many of those opportunities as possible. Even if you start with the simple things, they'll have a major impact on her.

For example, bread, salad, salad dressing, and wine can be powerful tools when used correctly. Here's an example scenario where an opportunity would exist to put your specific information about your sweetheart to work for you and certainly impress her. For the following scenario we're going to use the previously mentioned items. Let's review them in greater detail before we begin the story. Make-believe that in your workbook you've learned she loves sourdough bread, and the end piece of the loaf is especially to her liking because it's the crispiest piece in the loaf. At the end of her workweek, she enjoys having a few glasses of red wine with dinner. Also noted in your workbook is her love for salad and her favorite dressing—honey mustard, served on the side. Once you've gotten to know their likes and dislikes, the occasionally picky women are the best and easiest types to please. So if your sweetheart always orders her salad dressing on the side, remember it well.

Here is what you'd benefit from remembering about your woman in the case of the scenario you are about to read:

Freshly baked sourdough bread is her favorite, especially the crispy end. She likes to enjoy some merlot with dinner at the end of her workweek. She loves salad with honey mustard dressing ordered on the side.

Imagine you're going to pick up your little lady from work. You arrive at her downtown office building right on time. But you find she's running a half hour to an hour behind schedule. It's a Friday night and the drive home in rush-hour traffic is always undesirable. You know she's going to be hungry and tired—just as you are. Instead of getting worked up about the delay, you peek into the cozy little café directly across the street from her office building.

You decide both of you would fare better by unwinding over dinner instead of sitting in traffic starved and grumpy. Upon entering the café you discover it has a small gift shop inside. You still have at least 40 minutes until she clocks out, so you look around a bit. Suddenly you begin to feel sympathetic toward your honey for having to work such a long day in what has been a seemingly never-ending and stressful week for her.

Being the kind, sensitive, thoughtful man you are—or are in training to be—you decide to have a couple of beers and watch a little *Sports Center*. Oh no, you don't. Not until after you've taken care of business first. Strolling around the gift shop, you manage to put together a nice gift basket to surprise your sweetie. Then you ask the server to prepare a romantic candlelit table for two. Meanwhile your hardworking honey probably dreads the moment she'll be asked what she wants to do for dinner, what and where to eat, not to mention she's bound to feel lousy about you having had to wait so long for her. Little does she know, you've since had a gift basket wrapped for her, drank a cold beer and watched a bit of hockey—hey, your workweek wasn't exactly an easy one either.

You phone her and tell her when she is done with work you want her to call you from her cell phone when she is standing outside the front of her office building. She thinks you'll be driving around front to pick her up. But the truth is, that's when you cue your waitress to bring out the items you've pre-ordered. You're not quite certain of what your sweetheart will be in the mood to eat—unless in your earlier phone conversation you were sharp enough to ask her—so you play it safe and order her something you know she loves. Thanks to your workbook you know she always loves to eat a salad with honey mustard dressing, *on the side*, and freshly baked sourdough bread.

Through the window of the restaurant you can perfectly see where she exits her office building. She has no idea where you've been waiting or what you've planned for her. Then your cell phone rings. It's she. "Where are you?" she asks. That's when you signal the waitress to bring out the piping hot sourdough bread, salad, and side of honey mustard dressing. You also order a couple glasses of merlot to help bring her workweek to a nice close. Continuing your telephone conversation, you instruct your guest of honor to walk directly across the street and enter the café. When she enters, she sees you sitting at a candlelit table for two. The dinner, wine, and gift have all been arranged to honor her.

You stand tall when she enters the room, and like a true gentleman does, you draw her chair and seat her at the table. Reaching into the basket of piping hot sourdough bread, you remove and place upon her plate the heel piece. Just then she begins to notice more of her favorite things you've taken the time to remember. In all her delight she sends you a smile that surely classifies you as her most favorite of them all—maybe even her dessert.

That was an example of what you can do by knowing just a few things desirable to your mate. The more information you have, the faster and better you'll get to know the woman with whom you're in love. Some people say, "It's impossible to get to know someone in every way." In one way they're right, we can't possibly remember everything about our partners. But that's still no excuse not to try. We can only know as much about a loved one as we are willing to try to find out about them.

Now you can have your *Gentlemen, Start* Her *Engine* book and workbook filled with nothing short of powerful and useful information about your special someone. What will you do with this material? I hope you don't think it can improve your relationship simply by filling it out, reading it once, and then retiring it to the bottom of your sock drawer or atop a dusty shelf. Because in all honesty that approach makes even less sense than a judicial system that sentences a criminal to 500 years in prison. So review and study your workbook occasionally. Try leaving it in your porcelain library.

Now that you know why and when you can convert and engage your two improved human senses, to do so regularly can begin to make you increasingly aware and more knowledgeable of the things you can do to stimulate your significant other's sense of romance, passion, security, and approval. Let's review what you should be learning from this chapter by taking a short quiz.

Circle the correct answer for each question below:

1. **What should men consider the two most essential human senses for increasing their awareness of the women in their lives?**
   a. Taste and touch
   b. Hearing and sight
   c. Smell and tell

2. What should men rebuild their sense of hearing into?
   a. A sensor for listening to a woman carefully
   b. A wireless network
   c. A Buddhist temple

3. What is a great opportunity for men to be all ears—listening to and watching their woman closely?
   a. Between plays when watching sports on the television
   b. Dinner dates
   c. When the paramedics and fire engine are forcing them to pull over

4. What is one form of flattery women appreciate most from a man?
   a. When he immediately falls asleep after climaxing and leaves her hanging again
   b. A man's ability to provide her with the things she likes, needs, and wants with rarely ever needing to ask her
   c. A man's ability to return home (happy) from his trip to the supermarket where his honey sent him to buy her a super value pack of extra absorbent feminine products and a tube of vaginal cream that needed a price check

5. What should men rebuild their sense of sight into?
   a. X-ray vision
   b. A sensor for watching a woman closely
   c. Boob-tube radar

6. When a man and a woman are together on a dinner date, out for a drink, or some other "quality time," what kind of contact must the man make when the woman is speaking to him?
   a. Physical contact
   b. Eye contact
   c. Contact his attorney

7. While a man and his sweetheart are on a date of any kind, what kind of distractions does the man want to avoid?
   a. Eating or drinking
   b. Quiet intimate settings
   c. Televisions, newspapers, magazines, work-related materials, and excessive people-watching

8. What is one definite precursor for a woman to develop lasting trust in her man?

> a. When he always goes out of his way to please his secretary and the other women in his office, but rarely makes an effort to please his honey at home
> b. When she recognizes he has a devoted interest in her, and she can begin to feel more secure about his love for her
> c. When he gives her a credit card with no limit.
> (This is not a trick question.)

9. What can a man do to start making it highly visible to the woman he loves that he has a deeply devoted interest in her?

> a. Wait until after the football season is over to finish reading this book
> b. Complete and properly use this book and its workbook section to create practical ways to express a devoted interest in a woman
> c. Wait until there aren't any beautiful women around for him to look at and then start paying attention to his sweetheart

(The answers to questions 1 through 9
are b, a, b, b, b, b, c, b, b.)

CHAPTER 4

TUNE-UPS AND TRACK CONDITIONS

Always Know What You're Up Against and How It Can Affect Your Race Pace

On the subject of romance and relationships, I've had discussions with a variety of men and women from all walks of life. As a result of my many discussions I've learned there are far more men than women who could use a tune-up in this particular area of life we call romance. So what is romance, how does it evolve, why does it seem to never last, why can't certain people appreciate it, and how come it can't save a marriage? In the relationship race your answers to the above questions are what determine your track conditions. In this chapter I hope to unlock and open many hearts to inherit the broadest appreciation, understanding, and meaning of romance there is.

It doesn't surprise me so many men still think to be romantic is universal in its form and expression. Men also can perceive romance to be too much work. To say the least, these interpretations of romance are grave misconceptions. When I speak to women in private, many of them tell me they don't feel special or desirable to their mate. Many women also admit not being satisfied by their mate's efforts and attempts to continue to keep them happy and feeling cherished.

Most men's attempts to be romantic are often seen by women as impersonal, thoughtless, and recognizably done at the last minute—and reserved for special occasions only. Rarely have I come across a woman who tells me her guy is anything but short of being a stud who knows how to push all the right buttons. But when I do meet a woman who speaks adoringly about her man, she has *many* delightful things to say about him, not just a few. It's obvious the men these women speak so highly of do something totally different than all of the other men who women say *just don't get it.*

There are some key characteristics I've noticed about the men who happen to be keeping their women in heaven. Once again metaphorically speaking, these men can cruise the course with their eyes shut, they know the track like the back of their hands, they are one with the automobile, and they possess what many of us call a home-field advantage. In other words these guys are experts in the areas and subjects pertaining to the women in their lives.

The women who are so romantically satisfied, clearly recognize the traits that set their guys apart from the majority of other men. These women, packed with self-esteem, tell me they constantly experience rewarding feelings like pride, flattery, and arousal, often good enough to brag about to their girlfriends. The bragging isn't about the things they get or how much they cost; it's more about their man's ability to know exactly the things they need and love to receive. Remember the one form of flattery most appreciated by women is a man's ability to provide them with the things they like, need, and want with rarely needing to ask them. That's proof enough for me, as well, as it should be for you. There are some definite advantages in knowing all you possibly can about the woman in your life.

"When a woman is made to feel special, he who has braved to deliver her splendor, will be bound by her favor."

—Steven A. Guerrero

So for the rest of the men, what is romance? Well, in general, romance for a lot of people it seems, is still being defined inappropriately. Daily, we are visually subjected to the examples and images of romance as portrayed on television, in motion pictures, and by some longhaired buff dude who can't pronounce the word butter. And so we continue to be force-fed impressions of a universal style of romance, causing many of us to think it must be that way in order for us to experience it to the fullest. Sadly there are many women yearning for any kind of attention, causing them to settle for even the slightest token gestures of this canned type of romance.

You might ask, "Why is it so important for men to learn how to satisfy a woman's appetite for romance?" Because when a woman is deprived of romance and attention, similar to food depravation, her eyes become bigger than her stomach. Therefore, anything with a hint of romance begins to look palatable to her. Studies have shown that if you do your grocery shopping when you're hungry, everything on the store shelves looks good and thus finds its way into your shopping cart. Like the grocery shopping theory, if your mate is hungering for romance, attention, appreciation, and affection, it can make her, in more ways than one, extremely vulnerable. Now her romance (shopping) cart will begin to overflow.

Much of what she is exposed to that depicts romance can heavily influence the romantic behavior she'll want to receive from her partner. That could make this book hazardous to some. He, however, often claims the behavior she expresses a desire for is uncharacteristic of his abilities.

> *"A man passes the test of love only when his willingness to please erases the myths of inability he has written within himself."*
>
> —Steven A. Guerrero

37

The one-size-fits-all philosophy rarely applies to romance, because romance is simply the method of how one determines what is to be given. Whether it's a gift, action, or affection, it's the amount of thought you put into it that your honey will appreciate the most. Women are experts in recognizing how much thought goes into what men do for them. When your lady can tell a lot of thought went into something you've done for her, look out because women love to be interesting to men.

When your lady can trust that you have a profound interest in her, she'll glow with confidence. There is nothing more attractive to men than a confident woman. In upcoming chapters you'll learn in detail how you can make everything you do for the woman you love assure her you have a devoted interest in her. Thereafter, no matter what you do for your honey, she should perceive it and you as romantic.

How romantic you are considered by your mate is determined by how much of your own thought goes into making her feel interesting. When applied correctly my method of romance can fulfill the unique areas of the recipient, not a mere one or two categories in the life thereof.

Fortunately, you only need to find out what the woman in your life needs and perceives as romantic behavior. If the things you learn to do for her, positively move her in anyway, you have begun to create romance. Does it sound romantic to you to watch a man clean a toilet or a bathroom? Of course not, because you're a man.

But ask a woman how it would make her feel to see a man polishing the latrine for her and you'll get an entirely different answer like, "My husband cleans the bathroom for me. He's so sweet." It stands to benefit men incredibly if they first learn exactly what the women in their lives are like and why they have the needs and desires they do. Then men can more successfully determine the kinds of things to give to and do for their sweethearts. How, you ask? Take a look at what I found to be the best definition in short that describes romance: *Romance: To try to influence favor with especially lavishing personal attention, gifts, or flattery* (from Merriam-Webster online).

So you need to be more of the romantic type? Then I suggest you learn how to get extremely personal with your significant other.

From my readings of many other definitions for the word romance, I've concluded it's no wonder men often associate romance with behavioral practices not within their ability to provide. These definitions primarily consist of words like prose, chivalry, adventurous, heroic, and mysterious.

So how's a guy supposed to know what kinds of personal things he can do to please his woman? How can he be sure his actions qualify as romantic loving behavior? Can he be confident his continuous efforts will sweep his beloved off her feet for years to come? How will his being selfless benefit him? In my eyes and many women's as well, there is only one correct answer to those questions, customized for the woman in question. It is to learn how to choose and use the right fuel for the right engine. This book will provide you with the proper fuel, how to use it, and why it should be your fuel of choice.

Just as a car engine requires fuel before you can even start it, your honey's particular style of engine requires a specific type of fuel. The right fuel will get her engine started and keep it running smoothly. Once you know the type of fuel she appreciates most, you can keep her tank full. You'd never put diesel fuel in the Ferrari, would you?

Gentlemen, there is a direct connection here I hope you understand. You see, unlike the glove boxes of automobiles around the globe, women have yet to come equipped with a care and maintenance manual. This has left men terribly disadvantaged—until now. This book will enable you to be knowledgeable about your partner's needs and desires and know how to easily fulfill them.

Here's romantic behavior in a nutshell—any action taken by the man meant especially for his lady, including but not limited to helping her, providing for her, listening to her, respecting her, acknowledging her, serving her, complimenting her, being considerate of her, learning about her, being supportive of her, and showing an interest in her.

When you begin to provide more and more of the things relative to your mate's desire and needs she can begin or continue to see you in a positive light. Then she can start to feel more secure, loved, appreciated, cherished, respected, and confident. From then on her trust in you will likely be inevitable. Subsequently, you'll begin to look and sound more delicious to her. Pardon my expression, but that's how it works.

Certainly her respect for you and your needs can increase substantially, as should her desire and willingness to engage in sexual intimacy with you more often. How much more often, you ask? Hmm. Just imagine if I had (in pill form) the answer to that question for you and millions of other men. To see how she'll be affected by your loving efforts and therefore respond to you lovingly, this time you'll need to let faith and patience be your guides. Without them it's impossible to succeed. Motivating yourself to strengthen and beautify the relationship with the woman you love requires more than removing a safety seal. As for your ability to succeed, it does not await you under some annoying clump of cotton. It's your sheer commitment to improve and stay accountable that will help ensure your relationship's success.

Because every woman is so unique in character and chemistry, determining how much more often your partner wishes to pursue sexual intimacy depends on many factors. One thing is for sure, if— and I mean a big if—her emotions are in proper alignment and intimacy does occur, it can be intensely satisfying for both of you— if you know what you're doing. So be careful, because despite her cries of ecstasy leading you to believe you know what you're doing, it doesn't always mean you do. But don't be offended. It's a known fact a staggering number of women fake orgasm and continue to do so until—sometimes forever. It's tragic. However, by simply asking your sweetheart a few intimate questions pertaining to her anatomy, it never has to be that way.

I would like to share with you the greatest tidbit of lovemaking advice I ever received that has since proven to be effective in my own marriage. While you may not be in need of this advice, it never hurts to be 100 percent sure. Simply ask your sweetie to show you exactly where her clitoris is located. Now don't laugh or be embarrassed. You'd be shocked at the number of men (even women) who are in the dark about this little light switch. Preferably, when you ask her, do it in private. Anywhere else could result in your being shown the back of her hand. Even worse you could end up in a jail cell if she decides to accommodate your request during church night bingo. In the event she doesn't even know where her clitoris is located, get to a bookstore immediately. Buy a book (with pictures) on the female sexual anatomy or genitalia. She will be eternally grateful to you.

Try not to be shy so you can get a good look at it up close—in-your-face close. But before you attempt to ask her this, there is a word of caution. If out of nowhere, leaps a request for a visual inspection of your little Mrs. Grundy's "gear box," she could interpret the inquiry as the solicitation of a perverted peep show. Now all of a sudden she suspects your late-night web surfing searching new investment strategies and hot deal vacations are anything but innocent.

Timing is everything if she is going to be able to recognize your attempt as a sincere effort to learn a priceless bit of information about her anatomy. A better time to ask her for this tour of her genitalia is when the two of you are preparing to make love. If you're still absolutely certain she'll have none of that, then the only suggestion I have left for you is www.EverythingAboutFemaleSexOrgansAndHow ToStimulateThem.something, with visuals. Educating yourself in this area is the first step of many toward helping you to help your honey reach the peaks of ecstacy when you make love to her.

When you're able to locate and identify her clitoris, kindly ask her to tell you and show you why, what, where, when, and how to manipulate it in ways that feel good to her. Massaging it, nibbling it, or tap dancing on it—just make sure you discover what it takes to stimulate her clitoris in such a way she can reach orgasm. And don't forget it's a finesse thing you're striving for here. Race car drivers don't just slide the key into the ignition and slam their foot, full throttle, down on the accelerator, do they? Oh no, it's a far more gentle and patient process than that. Warming up her engine is critical. So don't be offended if your sweetheart prefers the foreplay begin with the soft, slow, gentle persuasion of your finger or tongue instead of immediately mounting herself upon her supercharged stud.

Gentlemen, the results are in and what researchers discovered is this: An exceedingly high percentage of women studied—80 percent or more—were unable to experience a clitoral orgasm while engaged in vaginal intercourse. For the majority of women this happens to be the most intense and undisputed orgasm of choice. Unless the woman's clitoris is stimulated directly, the man will continue to be the first one to snore. Again, for most women to successfully climax, targeted clitoral manipulation before and during intercourse was found to be the overwhelmingly desired and most successful technique.

Absolutely, positively never assume you know what to do with the clitoris. More importantly, don't think rubbing it faster, longer, and harder will get you two wishes. Yes, I know it's usually three wishes, but in this case it's only fair the poor woman gets a wish for herself—to wish you would stop before she catches fire. The sexual advice I've just finished sharing with you was all I ever needed to be told. Granted it wasn't explained to me quite so vividly. Nonetheless, I still became very motivated, confident, and successful in my attempts to completely satisfy my wife in the area of this particularly important aspect of lovemaking—the orgasm. Furthermore, I'm not embarrassed to say (well, maybe just a little) I failed to learn this clitoral lesson until I myself was 25 years of age. Nonetheless I'm grateful to have discovered it when I did and if a similar case exists in your relationship, you and she will be just as grateful.

Prior to men being allowed to marry, I think they should be required to enroll in and pass a simple female anatomy course. Every woman deserves to be satisfied sexually by her mate. I hope this little bit of advice can get you and your significant other off in the right direction (pun intended). By completing this transformation into becoming the knowledgeable, more attentive, and faithful servant of her clitoris, exploring the rest can be easy not to mention fun when discovering.

Mark my words, making sure the woman in your life continues to experience the pleasure of orgasm will have some overwhelmingly positive effects on your relationship. However, you mustn't disregard her desire to keep up or not to keep up with the *pace of the race*, which in many cases can be determined by two factors. These two factors can also be responsible for your track conditions being hazardous or optimal. The track conditions created by these two factors are well within a man's ability to control. You could even say, "good or bad, a man paves his own road."

What I mean by *the pace of the race* is that an emotionally healthy woman's desire to willingly embrace and share her passionate, uninhibited sensuality with a man can frequently be determined by these two factors:

♥ Factor 1, his ability to keep her tank full with the proper type of fuel, can substantially increase her desire for sexual intimacy. In other words, he must reassure her of his interest, love, and support by doing and providing the things she needs and loves, thus increasing trust and her pace in the race.

♥ Factor 2, his showing a lack of interest in her by not keeping her tank full of the proper fuel, can substantially decrease her desire for sexual intimacy and possibly her caring to initiate it ever again. She feels treated like a token. As for the needs she has expressed being important to her, they have been ignored and by his standards considered ridiculous. This is a surefire way to evoke her difficulty in trusting him.

In addition to these two factors there are other situations that can occur in people's lives and you should be aware of them. These issues can be traumatic and difficult to control, and can stifle one's ability to ever achieve a healthy relationship. The effects these issues alone can have on track conditions are devastating. Until these issues are resolved, they have the potential to bring the relationship race to a screeching halt. They are the following:

♥ Sexual abuse   ♥ Substances abuse
♥ Sexual assault   ♥ Infidelity
♥ Domestic violence   ♥ Neglect
♥ Child abuse   ♥ Family of origin
♥ Mental abuse   ♥ Divorce
♥ Verbal abuse

Sadly, many people encounter one or a combination of abusive issues during their lifetime. Equally sickening is the percentage of individuals currently being affected by some form of abuse. If an individual lets such traumatic issues go unresolved, if they are never dealt with properly, his or her inability to function successfully within a relationship is frequently the result. Relationships do sometimes become volatile and dysfunctional. One of the most destructive behavioral patterns produced in these unhealthy dysfunctional relationships is the inability to appreciate anyone, even someone who is a great provider in every sense of the word.

In a normal relationship, factor 2 mentioned earlier doesn't require clinical services to be achieved. It is realistically within most men's capabilities to control and improve by their own recognizance. However, if a man continues to neglect his mate, he may be left with no other choice but to seek marriage counseling. And if one or more of the traumatic issues mentioned previously is involved, I highly recommend seeking the help of a professional. Indeed, this book cannot make bad things go away. Before my suggestions will improve your relationship, you and your partner must not be suffering abuse or the effects from it in the past. In order for peace and harmony to prevail within your relationship, both of you must have complete closure with any emotional traumas.

This book was never intended to mend a broken spirit—a broken heart, yes. Ideally the book will help to prevent many broken hearts as well. But not until the green flag is waving. In the sport of auto racing, waving the green flag indicates the racetrack is clear of all debris from an accident, assuring the racers they can proceed safely. When your track is clear, you can begin to pump the right fuel into her tank. The right fuel will race through her veins the same way it does through the fuel line of an automobile engine.

Good fuel helps maintain and increase the efficiency of other components essential for prolonging her passion to remain in the race. If you don't keep her tank full with the right fuel or you continue to fill it with the wrong fuel, you—and your relationship—could end up in the pits. By then you'll be getting closer and closer to being disqualified from the relationship race.

Before you put the blame on your machine, remember this: "Only a poor workman curses his tools." To get her engine started is one thing, but to keep it revving long and strong is another.

CHAPTER 5

DRIVER'S SCHOOL

Prepare to Race—and Know Your Course

In order for a man's relationship to receive maximum benefit from the use of this book, he needs to understand the reason(s) he has chosen to read it in the first place. Why? Because his reasons can determine the difficulty or ease of the course that lies ahead of him. As a result he must be willing to accept the course he has laid out for himself. The degree of urgency for improvement can vary from relationship to relationship, based on the woman's emotional condition. A gentleman's situation could be to one extreme, negative, or to the other extreme, positive. He may even find his relationship falls somewhere between the two extremes.

Let's look at an example of a man in the extreme negative situation. For instance, let's say the reason he's reading this book is because he's been the negligent one in his relationship—and by no means is that impossible to imagine. He continuously neglected his responsibility to please his honey. Now he and she are idling at the fork in the road. Thanks to him, she can't take it anymore. So if things don't start to get better pronto she'll end the relationship. All of a sudden he's ready to try. And all throughout the years his lovely wife has been telling him how uninteresting, unimportant, disrespected, overworked, undesirable, unappreciated, and taken for granted she has felt. But did he listen? No.

Whatever his reasons were for not trying, it wasn't important to him to strengthen the bond between him and his wife. Consequently, he's now sitting face-to-face with a marriage and family counselor and carries the business card of a divorce attorney in his pocket. Because of his honey's ultimatum and his counselor's recommendation (not to mention his attorney's projection) he's off to the bookstore. In a situation like his, it could take a while before he begins to notice improvements in his relationship. He can also expect to work harder than the men who didn't need an ultimatum to motivate them to improve. Let's just say he might have to "eat crow" for a while. How long? That depends on his ability to swallow every bite of the black feathered fowl with a smile.

What in the world does it mean to "eat crow"? My father's humble definition was that of being persecuted by a woman. What he really meant, and I eventually learned, was, "When you're guilty of a heinous love crime, the woman you've hurt reserves the right to see your deeds punishable by eating something far less mouthwatering than crow—and then you die." Thank you, God, for instilling such resiliency in the woman, and for giving some men a second, third, and maybe even a fourth chance to make things right with their sweethearts.

Something else you should prepare to handle patiently is when you and your partner are on love's road to recovery, the response time you can expect from her can vary. How soon you'll see a positive response will depend largely in part on how badly she was hurt and for how long she endured her suffering. Even after you've begun to care for her in the way she's needed you to all along, remember the amount of time for her healing process can occur proportionately to the severity and the length of time in which she suffered.

So if you've been a demolition driver, you might have to wait awhile, really developing a taste for crow, before she begins to trust you and your intentions again. When she is convinced you possess an undeniable commitment to please her, she can then trust her vulnerability is safe in your hands.

A more desirable reason for a man to find himself reading this book is because he received it as a gift. Perhaps his already "happy" wife is the one who chose this gift for him. Although she has never been one to complain and believes her husband is the kind of man with whom she can remain forever married, it can't hurt him to learn to be a little more romantic and attentive. If this is your situation, let me express my respect for you. Doing your best to be an accountable husband, keep your wife happy, and set a good example for your children are very admirable achievements.

From this point forward your marriage can only get better. But I do have a few words of caution for you. Happy, healthy marriages and relationships are like an overcast day at the beach without sunscreen. Just because you can't see the sun doesn't mean you aren't getting burned. By the time you realize it, your caboose is cooked. Because the overcast sky fails to keep the sun's most harmful, ultraviolet rays from penetrating the earth's atmosphere, we're still in danger of damaging our skin.

You see, complacency is to love, what carcinogens are to cancer. Similar to the way a person can get burned by the sun's incognito rays, unaware of the damage until it's too late, a peaceful marriage with complacent spouses can often lead to divorce. I'm sure these next few phrases sound familiar to you. "Over the years we just grew apart from each other." "He was nice and I loved him dearly, but I eventually outgrew him intellectually." And here's my favorite: "Of course I love her, I'm just not *in love* with her."

There are many cases where peacefully but not happily married couples divorce after 10, 15, or even 25 years together. And guess what? They never saw it coming.

Why do you suppose, in the beginning, a man cares for a woman like he docs a brand-new car? Soon thereafter why does she begin to feel and in some cases look like a run-down 1976 Pacer? I call it the lemon syndrome. According to most men, there are many reasons this lemon syndrome occurs. A few of the reasons can be justified, but most of them are sour grapes.

You see the majority of us men would really like to believe we simply "got a lemon." Metaphorically speaking, almost any man will tell you when he first drove her off the lot she was precious and purred like a kitten. She really had some get-up-and-go back then. And she looked so pretty parked in his driveway, where every week he'd proudly take care of her from top to bottom. He'd wash and dry her, wax her, check her fluids and tire pressure, and every 3,000 miles she'd get a lube and tune. He always took proper care of her.

Well, most of us know what happens when the novelty of a new car wears off. Once the odometer reads 30,000, 50,000, 80,000, or rolls into the six digits, the car is lucky to get the manufacture's recommended scheduled tune-up let alone some fresh oil and new filters. As for the car being cleaned and pampered, those days are long gone. Some cars only get cleaned when filling up their tank comes with a free drive-through quickie car wash. Naturally, that's when things begin to go wrong with any automobile. When it comes to cars, few individuals get stuck with a lemon. And if a consumer does in fact drive a lemon off the lot, there is a law, appropriately named "the Lemon Law," that protects the rights of the consumer.

When a man believes his honey is a lemon, what might that make him? A lemon tree? Unlike money, lemons do grow on trees. Would you agree that when a man falls in love with a woman, she is far from being a lemon to him? However, if she was a sourpuss (don't even go there) in the beginning, he must have loved her acerbic personality or he wouldn't be with her today.

When it comes to relationships, there is no lemon law. There are only lawyers, some of whom theoretically could be considered lemons by their ability to leave a taste in one's mouth so sour he or she would fare better and be wealthier to find a way to turn his or her situation back into a sweet one.

Do you ever feel like you've ended up with a woman who you just can't figure out a way to please? If your answer is "yes," I have some questions to ask you before you continue to try or give up on your relationship. Do you believe you've tried everything possible to improve your relationship and still nothing has worked? How much and what have you really tried to find out about your partner? How much time have you spent trying to figure her out? Do you know how to locate and then provide what her needs and desire are and why you should? Do you know and understand why she is different from other women? Do you keep track of the things that make her happy? If you don't keep track or document any of the information pertaining to her needs and desires, how do you remember them—your memory? Do you know what you can do with what little you already know about her?

Your answers to the previous questions have a lot to do with the current track conditions you're experiencing in your relationship—bad or good. If you've been trying to rely solely on your memory to retain useful information about your sweetheart, it's no wonder you're tired and frustrated, and suffer from a forget-about-it attitude. Doesn't it make sense to try some easy suggestions that truly have the ability to help you steer clear of a breakup (or a breakdown) with the woman you love?

This book is loaded with the truth about everything from cars to lemons to women and sadly even about why some women will choose a ride on a Harley over their husbands. But I have left the many truths about your special someone for you and her to discover in the workbook. No one else can do it except you and her. Then you can say your book is loaded with the truth, the whole truth, and nothing but the truth about the woman you love.

CHAPTER 6

RACING TO WIN

Don't Crash and Burn

In a sport like auto racing the term "crash and burn" is not taken lightly. Usually a "crash" is the result of a poorly executed maneuver, an overly aggressive attempt to pass an opponent, or some freak malfunctioning of the car. Smack into the wall they go, sometimes bursting into flames. The word "burn"—as in third degree—speaks for itself . When a race car driver is in a crash moving at speeds in excess of 220 miles per hour, his chance of survival is for the most part, out of his hands.

Most drivers emerging from a wreckage alive and in one piece, although unable to finish the race, won't think twice before getting behind the wheel of their machine to race again. And just like before, the race car driver will race to win. Do you race to win in your relationship? Can you continue racing to win even after you've had a horrible crash?

If you always try your best to do the things your woman loves and needs you to do, you're doing what I call racing to win. However, if you're just joining in the race, be aware that even when you do all the right things for your sweetheart, there will be times when she won't jump for joy or even notice. I know it's not fair and that's why I've decided to call it a crash. A crash occurs when, prior to a man doing his good deed(s), he has made up his mind exactly how he wants his mate to respond to his kindness. Much to his disappointment her response is weak or, worse yet, she may not respond at all. Can you hear the tires skidding, followed by a short silence and then *crash?* The more you do for your loved one the more you may feel an increase in the need for her to show her appreciation for the things you do. And that's quite all right, it's normal for anyone to feel that way. You can also find, in return for meeting your sweetheart's needs and desires so greatly that your expectations of her to provide for your needs can increase almost simultaneously.

My wife admits that once in a while she forgets to thank me for things I do for her. She also confesses to occasionally being too tired for a few laps around the track with me even though I feel like I've just gotten a tune-up. Sometimes she can walk right past something I've done for her and not even notice or maybe she'll notice but doesn't make a big deal out of it. For whatever reasons, occasionally it happens, and sometimes it can hurt. Thankfully it's only occasionally.

For the sake of my marriage, I've learned that when there is a crash, getting mad and letting my wife know is the surest and quickest way to crash and burn. If I want to continue racing to win I cannot let myself burn with anger or disappointment. So to keep myself from getting totally bent out of shape, I tell myself this: "I can always recover from a crash, which almost always is a minor fender bender, if I don't turn it into a major wreck." Because if I let myself burn, there is a good possibility I, my wife, our kids, and our marriage will be terribly scarred, possibly even totaled. As long as I know I've given my best and raced a good race, I remain proud of myself for not being a quitter.

Another thing that helps me avoid the burn is respect of my wife's right to be human. The minute I forget she is human, the reasons I do all the things I do for her are lost in selfishness. She never forgets that I'm also entitled to be human, which helps to keep me doing for her purely out of love. There isn't enough paper in the world to fill a book with all the wonderful things she does for me. Okay, so I'm exaggerating a little bit, but if you could also learn to stretch the *good* truth at the right times, you'd soon discover the wonderful benefits that can occur as a result.

Out of all the things you choose to do for your significant other, you'll probably find the ones most pleasing to her are the ones you're not accustomed to doing. In the beginning, when doing anything you're not accustomed to doing, you may feel out of place, embarrassed, degraded, or not very manly (ouch!), but it won't last long. You might be more susceptible to uncomfortable feelings when doing things that require your "sensitive side" or what you've always thought was a "woman's job." You might—no, you *will*—catch some flack from your male friends and family, possibly your own dad. But your honey should be willing to express enough gratitude toward you to eliminate any fear of becoming a sissy or a pushover. You'll be laughing your "kiss-ass" self all the way to the bedroom and maybe even other rooms in the house—while those other defiant fellows are....

The woman you love will be very happy to notice you've begun to understand her needs and are trying to fulfill them. But just like everything else we start out being crazy about, over time her excitement for the things you're doing may dwindle. Then you might begin to feel like it's no longer worth the effort if she isn't going to show her appreciation anymore. Don't worry, it's normal for humans to occasionally get lost in the shuffle. The abundance of responsibilities in our daily lives can lead us to forget how good we really do have it with our partners, thus getting used to their perks and quirks, but mostly the former.

Humans are notorious for becoming complacent with wonderful lifestyles. Men should not ignore it if their significant other never acknowledges their contributions or they're becoming smug about praising them. To the contrary, if you think your honey is taking you for granted and racing to win feels more like a demolition derby, I highly recommend you talk to her.

Don't approach her as if you are ready to "blow a piston." Simply begin by asking your sweetheart, in your very best "indoor voice," if she appreciates all the things you do. If despite your being a loving, helpful, romantic, and attentive man, her answer is still "absolutely not," it's time you took her show on the road. As good a place as any to start will be on trash TV shows—at least that way you can get paid for your misery.

If, however, her answer is, "Yes, of course I do," it will probably be followed by her asking, "Why, do you ask?" This is when you can begin to tell her gently and blamelessly how you're feeling.

Informing her that your feelings are hurt is a good place to start. Yes, it is okay for a man's feelings to be hurt. Nonetheless, when you express yourself to her, it's not okay for your hurt feelings to cause you to shell out words like "never," "always," "nothing," "everything," "worthless," and so forth. For example, "you never," "you always," "you do nothing," "I do everything," or "you're worthless." Those phrases convey absolute meaning. By directing them at her, you'll send a negative or insulting message. Her natural response will cause her to be defensive, which will in effect make the conversation useless.

On the other hand, do not avoid opportunities to use words with absolute meaning to send a kind, loving, and motivational message to your sweetheart. You have my approval to use phrases like "I've never loved anyone the way I love you," "I'll never give up on us," "I'll always love you," "you always look stunning," "you're always thinking of me," "there's nothing I'd like to do better then to be with you right now," and "nothing will ever stop me from loving you." Are you getting the picture? Remember that a marriage or relationship without loving expressions like those you've just read, could eventually become "meaningless."

I hope I've made you aware of some of the more frequently spoken handle-with-care words and phrases. Now you can lovingly ask your lady, without offending her, if she could please try to pat you on the back more often. You can explain to her how expressing her gratitude toward you helps to keep you motivated, is very appreciated, and emotionally gratifying.

I'll tell you what is extremely rewarding to me, yet sometimes I tend to let it go unrecognized. My wife rarely complains, if ever. And believe me if she wanted to she could find plenty of things to complain about. But for one reason or another she cuts me some slack for the same things I hear a lot of other women squawking about to the men in their lives.

The message my wife's rarity of complaining sends to me is this: Apparently she does recognize my efforts to please her and values them dearly. But even when I feel like I'm slacking off a bit, she keeps cool about it. Maybe it's because she's mature enough, diplomatic enough, and realistic enough to realize nobody can get to everything all the time.

My wife admits that for as long as she's known me, I've been a very romantic, giving, domesticated, attentive gentleman. She also refuses to take credit for the person I have grown to be. I, on the other hand, give her all the credit for making it so rewarding for me to continue racing to win. The truth is every man has the choice to be loving, caring, romantic, and attentive. Also, every woman has the choice to do her best to encourage a man to treat her special forever. I know it can be frustrating when happiness and progress continue to elude you despite your vigilance.

I can assure you, throughout my past relationships with different women, one of the things I learned is that the more a person does, the greater the risk of being taken for granted. However, one thing we mustn't forget is that our partner is human. Humans make mistakes. And sometimes humans forget that they tend to forget they are human. Of course, I'm not condoning any behaviors or actions that are immoral and unjust. When a man is diligently trying to please his woman, he can become easily discouraged if she repeatedly forgets to praise him for his effort.

If a woman repeatedly neglects her responsibility to acknowledge a man crash after crash will occur until he finally burns out. And what can happen next is not a good thing. But let's not forget, every human is entitled to make mistakes and be forgiven. Unfortunately there will still be times when you feel like you've "hit the wall." The difference between you hitting the wall and a race car hitting the wall is this: You have the ability to keep yourself from bursting into flames while the driver of the race car does not.

The race car driver risks his life every time he gets in his car to race. Yet, if he survives an awful crash, rarely does he quit racing.

You might call him crazy, but he is brave and passionate. He is in love with and committed to the sport of auto racing. You, on the other hand, could prematurely burst into flames of anger because your mate forgot to say "thank you." She may not always jump up and down happily when you've done something nice for her. Rewarding you by ripping your clothes off that same night and making sweet passionate love to you might not occur when you most expect it to. If you stop doing nice things for your lady for the reasons I've mentioned above or similar ones, you are not racing to win.

If, when you do something nice for your mate, you always expect a certain type of reaction, I can almost guarantee you won't get the reaction you're looking for. So don't set yourself up for what I might call the kamikaze crash and burn. Instead, try your best to do nice things for your beloved purely because you're passionate about her, you love her, you want to teach her, and you're crazy about making her happy. If you give and do for a woman purely because you love her, you shouldn't expect so much in return all the time. If you can master the art of unconditional giving, better and better things can eventually begin to happen for you.

So if you crash, and you will crash from time to time, that's the time to remember both you and your honey deserve the right to be human and make mistakes. If your sweetheart forgets to give unconditionally to you, or if she doesn't express the proper gratitude for something you've done, don't let yourself burn. Stop and ask yourself this question: "Would I rather be trapped inside a burning car, or not be thanked by my sweetheart occasionally and told 'not tonight, honey, I'm really tired'?" The choice is yours.

"When disappointment is the result of giving, a heart's intentions are unveiled —and better not to have been given."

—Steven A. Guerrero

CHAPTER 7

THE RIGHT FUEL FOR THE RIGHT ENGINE

Why Some Engines Keep on Knocking and What Can Be Done About It

Many a man at one time or another has been left standing confused. Scratching his head with one hand and holding flowers and a box of chocolates in the other. Flowers and chocolates he thought for sure were going to make his honey happy. But instead, she muttered, "Thanks. Just set them over there for now." Then she asks, "Can you please go get the clothes in the dryer and put them on the couch so I can fold them after I'm done with these dishes? By the way, did you remember to stop at the market for me to pick up some milk and eggs for the meatloaf I'm making for dinner tonight? What, you forgot again?" Oops. Guess whose eating flowers for dinner?

I've heard many romance experts swear (with good intentions) and I quote, "A man can't go wrong giving flowers or chocolate to a woman." Oh yes, he can. I know a lot of women who hate flowers and aren't crazy about chocolate either or are still in rehabilitation.

Over the years, many different things have lost their luster with women, such as flowers and chocolates. Offering to fold the laundry along with performing other domesticities, complemented by the ability to remember, especially when asked, to pick up some milk and eggs, have gained a widespread popularity as the new aphrodisiac for women. Leave the stereotypical romantic gestures for the rookies. Unless, of course, you know for sure your lady always loves to receive whatever it is you plan to give her. If that's the case, then by all means, flowers and chocolate it should be.

From now on it will be to your advantage to provide for your mate strictly based on the desires and needs she shares with you in the workbook section. Her past experiences, personal preferences, priorities, job circumstances, and household environment will help you develop a simple strategy that's sure to be effective. All of this information you can have documented in your workbook.

Understanding how certain daily circumstances can affect your woman, is the first step in learning how to choose the right areas to begin fulfilling her in. In Chapters 8, 9, and 10, I show you how to easily understand your mate's unique circumstances while giving you hundreds of easy ideas for how to satisfy her needs and desires successfully. By following my suggestions you'll be able to continue providing your honey with the right things at the right times. Hypothetically speaking, you'll be filling her tank with the right "fuel." Here are some circumstances I often found can determine the needs and desires of a woman and even cause them to change sometimes.

You don't need to answer these questions right now. You and your significant other will be asked to do so later on in the workbook. In questions 2, 3, 4, and 5, the word "work" relates to anything that is not considered leisure time. For example, cooking, cleaning, doing dishes, grocery shopping, tending to or helping children, maintaining pets, writing out the bills, doing laundry, ironing, and so forth. You get the idea.

1. What type of job or profession does she have? (full-time homemaker counts as a job)

2. How many days a week does she work?

3. How many hours a day does she work?

4. What time does she have to wake up to get ready for work or help others get ready?

5. What time does she return home from work or stop working at home?

6. How much time does she get at the end of the day for relaxing, doing absolutely nothing but resting?

7. How many children are you raising together?

Depending on both you and your honey's answers, the previous seven questions can help both of you pinpoint circumstances that are negatively affecting your relationship and why. Doing this helps tremendously in determining the areas where adjustments can and should be made. Consequently, when we neglect to make needed adjustments that without a doubt we are capable of, eventually the romance in our relationship diminishes rapidly and even becomes stagnant. It's the marital cancer. The following is a brief dramatization.

Shirley gets home from work at 7:00 P.M. Richard gets home at 5:30 P.M. yet he waits until Shirley arrives to eat because she has to make his dinner. If there was ever a recipe for resentment this one ranks pretty high. Richard is eventually going to complain about not eating supper until 8:00 P.M. every night. Richard's discontentment will make Shirley feel taken for granted. Wait a minute, there is a solution. Richard can make his own dinner and eat by 6:00, right? Wrong. We have some sayings in our house, "If you can do for you, you can do for two," and "If I can do for me, I can do for three." We live by those sayings.

If he wanted to be a stud in the previous dinner dilemma, Dick would take the initiative and see that dinner is prepared and served when Shirley gets home. (To make things easier for all the guys still eating Spam from the can, in Chapter 12, I offer great ideas for preparing quick, fresh, and delicious *no-cook* meals and desserts. Yes, in fact, this book is all-purpose.) Just remember to always prepare enough for two or as many mouths as there are to feed in your household. Whether or not you wait to eat with your honey, is up to you. She will still appreciate your having thought of her when her difficult day is through.

For a woman, there can be many things that shape and mold her idea of the type of man she is to fall in love with and eventually marry. Her preferences and expectations for romance and everyday interaction with a man are developed over a long period of time. So much of what women experience from the beginning of their childhood through adulthood can determine what they expect from and appreciate in a man. A woman's relationship with her father and the relationship she witnessed between her mother and father can often play a huge role in whether she becomes the mushy type, the rugged outdoor fly fisherwoman, or a combination.

I could go on for days, even weeks, explaining the many circumstances responsible for the development of a woman's perception of men and romance and how she acquired her needs, but we're dealing with *now*. So you can forget about tapping deep into the human psyche to trace your sweetie's past at a rate of 125 dollars $125.00 an hour starting when she was five.

In order for a man to romantically and emotionally fulfill a woman forever, depending on her engine style, there will be specific ways and times in which he must accommodate her needs if he's to succeed. One of the questions I'm often asked by men is, "How am I supposed to know the specific ways and times to provide?" Before I give you the answer, I'll tell you the reasons why so many men don't know the specific ways or times to provide for their ladies. The reasons are, if you'll pardon my expression, manifold. The first reason is they have yet to take the time or make the effort to learn the specifics about their ladies. The second reason is they mistakenly think there has to be a reason or special occasion to do something nice for their honey. And the third reason is they don't know the myriad things they could do because they haven't done the first thing.

Now here's the answer to the question for specific ways and times a man can provide for his sweetheart. The happiest women in the world admit the men in their lives are well aware every day offers an opportunity to display their love and affections for their ladies. All throughout the weeks, months, and years these men recognize constant causes for celebration, recognition, and expressions of appreciation for their women and the things they love. I hope I've made it clear enough about when it is appropriate to do something nice for a lady.

I'm not going to just leave you hanging with that brief explanation. I'll break it down for you further. Not knowing when, what, why, or how doesn't have to be the reason for not trying anymore. Of all the opportunities in which you can and should take some kind of action to express your love and gratitude for your mate, there are only three categories with which to concern yourself. I would be shocked to find a woman who wasn't elated by having these three categories fulfilled by the man she loves.

Each category perfectly defines the answer to the question, "How am I supposed to know the specific ways and times to provide?" By keeping these three categories in mind at all times, you can capitalize on them as often as you'd like. The three categories are as follows:

1. Just because
2. Surprise
3. Special occasions

Now I'll share with you a brief definition for each category.

Just Because

To women this category is also called "the everyday things a man does for her that say 'I love you' in a big way." This opportunity is available to men every day and doesn't involve diamonds or gold or trips to Spain—unless, of course, that's within your budget. Regardless of a guy's bankroll, if he reaches his full potential in this one area alone or comes anywhere near it, his honey can feel as though she's a queen in paradise and treat him like her king.

Surprise

One of the great things about a surprise is that it can be anywhere and anytime you imagine. When you arrange surprises, oftentimes the more unusual the place and least likely your sweetheart expects something from you, the better. What you surprise her with, when, where, and how you present it (using your workbook), is entirely up to you. Keep your surprises simple and you can forever stay consistent—that is the key. "You" can even be the surprise if she is not expecting you. However, if your wish is to maximize the impact your surprises have on your partner, you'll need to do a little homework to make sure you succeed. When you have completed the lists in your workbook, you'll have already done most of the research needed to plan an unsuspecting shocker, large or small, for your sweetheart.

When it comes to surprising my wife, I like to shoot for at least three times a month—even if it's only with a cut flower from our garden, a piece of her favorite candy, or a short love note I can sneak into her lunch pail before she leaves for work. Occasionally I address a card or love letter to my wife and mail it to her at work. Sometimes without her needing to ask me, I offer her a back scratch, shoulder or foot massage—after her rough day at work—and it comes as a pleasant surprise to her.

Special Occasions

Pleasing your partner just because and with an occasional surprise can keep your relationship strong, passionate and mysterious. But you can never forget the special occasion. Within this particular category there are eight occasions you'll want to remember. Even if you were never to have read this book, you'd still be expected to acknowledge your mate on these occasions, or else. Before we go any further, let's try to agree on one thing: It's a shame most women have to wait for these special events to be acknowledged:

1. Birthday
2. Christmas
3. Anniversaries
4. Valentine's Day
5. Mother's Day
6. Marriage proposal
7. Honeymoon
8. Retirement

Depending on your sweetheart, there could be more occasions she would enjoy your acknowledging: Easter, St. Patrick's Day, New Year's Eve, ethnic holidays, etc. But the above eight are the major ones.

Never think that just by doing something incredible for one or all eight of the above occasions you don't have to do anything for the other 357 days of the year. You'll get the best results if you're thoughtful throughout the entire year just because and you surprise her every now and then. Think of the just-because and surprise categories as foreplay. (What do you mean, "What's that?"!) Then when you do create a masterpiece for celebrating a special occasion, even if it's only once a year, it can turn out to be climactic for her and you both.

Special occasions don't need to involve weekend getaway trips, exotic vacations, or diamonds and gold as often as you might think. As a matter of fact, as long as what you do for your lover is personal, sentimental, and occasionally unexpected, you can make her feel honored and cherished. The key is to remember that the things you do for her should be all about her and the things she loves most.

When you've completed all the lists in your workbook, you'll know exactly what her style, needs, appreciations, and preferences are for today, tomorrow, and maybe even the duration of your life with her. Your goal is to be one who arranges something special for her retirement. Much of what you'll find from completing the workbook, many happy couples have already discovered as useful tools to create a healthy relationship and lasting romance. As well, in the workbook there are many other things you would have never thought could be used to encourage an environment where romance can flourish.

The knowledge you will soon possess about the woman you love, could be all you'll ever need to take care of her romantically and emotionally for a lifetime. In order to help you avoid those unnecessary trips to the florist and candy shop or wherever, I've created a unique and more accurate approach for you to adopt. My approach makes it simple for you to succeed from the start, so you can begin to see immediate results from your efforts. You will benefit by determining which of the following is your sweetheart's engine style.

Engine Style = Her Daily Lifestyle

1. *Diesel engine*—The working woman without children or whose children have grown and gone.

2. **Economy engine**—The working woman with children or the full-time homemaker with children.

3. **High-performance engine**—The full-time homemaker without children or whose children have grown and gone.

By now you should know which category applies to the woman in your life. With her engine style remaining your number one consideration, your workbook, when completed, will serve you better.

There will be a chapter individually devoted to each of the three engine styles. Regardless of which engine style your partner has, read through all three styles. The idea is for you to notice how the engine style of each woman can greatly benefit from getting the appropriate fuel. The engine style is symbolic of the woman's lifestyle. In the scenarios the things being done to accommodate the woman's specific needs and desires are symbolic of the fuel she requires to stay happily driven—and not the way you're thinking either. When you have completed the workbook, you'll have more fuel than a refinery.

Often your partner's daily lifestyle or drastic change thereof can determine her likes, dislikes, needs, and desires. It's also possible to witness a change in her priorities and preferences from years past. But this targeted approach is designed to work together with the workbook to minimize your chances of doing things that have little or no effect on her. In the workbook section there are 350 ways for you to supercharge your woman's heart. Since many of us men rarely stop to ask for directions when we're lost, I've designed the workbook to be used like a roadmap (hopefully with a little more success). And before you know it, you'll be right on course to please her—and in victory lane for good.

Under certain circumstances some women can be one engine style one week and another style the next. I'm speaking of the effects children from a previous marriage often present in a love relationship. Take my situation, for instance. Having joint legal custody of my daughter Jessica makes my wife Angelica an economy engine woman half the time and a diesel engine woman the other half. You see, depending on child custody arrangements, a parent's lifestyle can differ from time to time.

Divorcees who have stepchildren going back and forth between the parents' homes can expect changes in their household environment. One week your partner can be a working mother or stepmother. The following week she can be a working wife without children. If you don't have children going back and forth from your home, then I'm sure your mate fits into one of the three engine styles perfectly.

Another great quality of this book is the timeless design of its use. As your wife goes through changes in her life—having babies, changing jobs, children going off to college or to get married—this book provides you with a revealing look and profound understanding of all your possibilities. It enables you to develop a strategy best suited for you, your beloved mate, and the overall well-being of your relationship.

There is a good reason for determining which of the three engine styles is under the hood of your honey. It is so you can begin to grasp the relationship between the following:

1. Her engine style, and her needs and desires.
2. Why certain needs and desires have become more important and desirable to her than others.
3. Why some of her original needs and desires are subject to change completely in the future.

Frequently, I hear couples say, "After we were married, everything changed. We now have more responsibilities—kids, a career, household duties—and there just isn't any more time for fun and romance." I know it can be difficult to find time in a hectic schedule, but mark my words, we will never find time if all we ever do is look for it. We need to use the energy we're wasting on conjuring up the excuses for why we can't find the time—and put it toward creative ideas to make time.

Men can no longer afford to let the little things—and the not so little things—continue to go unprovided for their ladies. On the contrary, men must start learning what the most desirable and undesirable things (little or not) are to their mates and from that knowledge prove to them they are a team—equal on the playing field. By answering the seven critical questions (see Chapter 13) you can calculate the amount of free time you and your sweetheart have in the morning, during the day, and after work. It's a sure way to see your diplomatic mission begins fairly.

If men refuse to provide in the areas where they're needed most by their women, they can eventually get a rude awakening. If more men cleaned, did the laundry, prepared meals, ironed clothes, shopped for groceries, put dishes away, and so forth, those same relationships would benefit incredibly. You'll soon find that the little and not so little things come in many different forms and the benefits of learning to do them are immeasurable.

Certain things a man can do for a woman will relieve her of huge amounts of stress and can turn out to be the cure for the common complaint, known as, "I do everything for you around here and you never help me." That complaint is almost always the beginning of the end for romance and intimacy—or sex as it's called by many.

When a woman has a full-time job, there are still household duties that need to be taken care of and it shouldn't be her job to do them without help. One person should never be obligated to carry the entire household burden alone. You'd never expect your roommate/buddy to pick up after you, cook your meals, or do your laundry and grocery shopping. All you'd ever expect from them is to pay their portion of the rent and utility bills (on time), buy their own food, beverages, household and hygiene products, respect the place, and clean up after themselves, and you're happy. Most male roommates are very diplomatic when it comes to sharing household chores and responsibilities. They share the responsibility of doing nothing. These guys simply keep their refrigerator stocked with cold beer at all times and see to it the pizza fund remains in check. It's a filthy place yet a happy and peaceful one.

But there's something about an intimate relationship or getting married that for many men, changes things. All of a sudden he thinks he can impose upon his sweetheart a slew of ridiculous duties and expectations. Wrong.

Most of the time women don't ask too much of us men, they just want a little help, TLC, understanding, consideration, and appreciation. Because many of us men were pampered for so long by our mothers we have difficulty understanding why our significant other can't take care of us like our mommy did. There's the answer. She is not our mommy.

The Bible even says, "A man shall leave his mother and father and cleave to his wife." The verse doesn't say, "Cleave to all your mother did for you and dump it on your wife to do." When a man moves out of his parents' home and gets married, his beloved partner does not inherit the same role his mother assumed, while his 42-inch waist father hid in the garage pretending to fix something or sat around the television and did nothing.

Back in the days (*way back*) when most men were the only source of income in their homes, their wives could be found doing the cooking, housework, taking care of the kids, and picking up after the husband. Eventually, regardless of whether the woman was working a full-time job, raising children, or both—she was still expected to stay in her role as a "happy homemaker."

Today many women work hard at a full-time job, which generates additional and in some cases the entire household income. Nonetheless, many of these working women continue to face the same expectations as previous generations. When we live with a loved one, picking up after ourselves and chipping in around the house is the least we can do toward helping ease the overall household load.

Relationships are about sharing everything, not just the good things. Men's efforts should be aimed toward learning to recognize the areas where they can share their love, support, and service with their ladies, as needed. Once you have found the areas in the workbook where she needs you most, commit yourself graciously and unconditionally to provide your assistance to the best of your ability.

Now, get ready, because you're about to test-drive the scenarios of all three engine styles of women. But before you begin I must inform you that while reading through the scenarios you will notice the mood of the material becoming extremely romantic. Prepare yourself, because it won't be like anything you're used to reading in men's magazines. Due to the extreme nature of the considerate, attentive, and romantic behavior extended toward the women in all of the scenarios, you could feel as though things are all in their favor.

With that in mind, also know that you should never be expected to do all the things being done in the scenarios. I wouldn't want any of you to become a doormat. I'm simply inviting you to take a trip through the mind of a truly willing and romantic man who knows his woman in the most beneficial ways possible. And he himself, in numerous ways, is very fulfilled as a result.

While you're reading the scenarios, notice the things getting done for the woman, being provided for her, and being said to her. Also pay close attention to how the domestic duties and other actions performed apply to each individual engine style. Each scenario was constructed to offer men practical ideas they can use to provide for their sweethearts in the just-because, surprise, and special occasion categories.

The scenarios also show you how having your workbook completed can make it simple to be accurate and more consistent when you do anything for your woman. As a result of all the information you'll have documented about her in your workbook, your own creative ideas will begin to flow. And they will flow in ways complimentary to your lady's specific needs and desires. Almost immediately you can easily start to fulfill the requests and desires she has expressed. However, if you believe you're not the creative type, think again.

All of the scenarios you'll be reading throughout this book have actually occurred. Don't concern yourself with who is doing the good deeds in the scenarios. The characters in the scenarios are merely portraying men with a never-ending desire to please their partners. Instead, try to focus on the things being done to take care of and provide for the specific engine style of the woman in each scenario.

All of the things that take place in the scenarios are realistic for men to do or to have done for the women they love; I'm proof of that. You see, I've done nearly all of them for my wife at one time or another and quite a few of them I still do to keep her and me very happy and feeling loved to this very day. So get in, buckle up, hold on, and let's roll.

CHAPTER 8

THE DIESEL ENGINE WOMAN

The Working Woman Without Children or Whose Children Have Grown and Gone

The women in this category are employed full-time. They are married or living with their partner. These ladies have yet to bear children and may never choose to have them, or they're empty nesters (kids have moved out). Whatever the case may be, these women are career-oriented and work in every field imaginable.

Regardless of this woman's type of occupation or income, a full-time commitment is involved. In many cases she can be required to work numerous hours of overtime. And she can return home late, stressed out, hungry, and exhausted. Yet, in the case of our diesel-engine woman, there are no children in the relationship, which does simplify things tremendously. For these couples, not having children makes it easier to focus on their relationship and give 100 percent effort toward fulfilling the needs and desires of each other.

Under these childless circumstances, you and your sweetheart can enjoy the freedom of romantic privacy. Romantic privacy creates unlimited options in the areas of romance and creativity. So depending on the preferences of the diesel engine woman in your life—anything goes when it's just the two of you. But it does take more than surprise candlelit dim sum suppers at home to keep men from one day becoming *sum dum* guy to the ladies. However, women can remain continuously impressed by the previous dinner gesture if it's not the only thoughtful thing their men ever do for them.

In the following **"Just Because" Scenario**, be sure to pay special attention to the italicized elements. These are the creative ideas, nice things said, and good deeds done that will spark your own creativity. At the end of the first just-because scenario, I'll show you how the information was extracted from specific lists in the workbook in order to come up with the ideas. I'll give only one example in this chapter and for the just-because scenario, otherwise this book would have more pages than you would care to read. Besides, accessing information from your workbook for a just-because opportunity is exactly the same for a surprise and special-occasion opportunity.

A "Just Because" Scenario for the Diesel-Engine Woman

It's Monday, the alarm clock is going off at 4:00 A.M. like it will for the next four days in a row at the exact same time. Of all the things people do at this wee hour of the morning, even getting ready for work seems a little insane. You specifically get out of bed to *walk your sweetheart to her car,* which happens to be parked on the street in front of your condo. You live in a fairly safe neighborhood, but then again so did many of the world's missing persons. So with your honey's safety the main concern, you escort her to the car and watch her drive off. Keeping fit is very important to her so she remains dedicated to exercising. If she didn't make the time for her fitness routine at this hour of the morning, she would have to do it after she finished work. If that were the case, she wouldn't get home until after 8:00 P.M. and barely have time to take a shower and eat a small meal—much less have any quality time to spend with you.

She'll be back from her workout by 5:30 A.M., which is about the same time you finish getting ready for work. Then while she gets ready for work you *prepare some freshly ground coffee and fix breakfast.* You could just make breakfast for yourself but your wife is always on your mind. Besides, it takes about the same amount of time to prepare enough food for two meals as it does for one; anyway, she makes the bed every morning and you sleep in it too. Your expertise lies in messing up the bed not fixing it. You've made her coffee so many times, you *know what kind of cream and sweetener she loves and how much of it to put in her special coffee cup. Even if her special cup is dirty, you wash it, fill it with hot coffee, and deliver it to her with a smile and a kiss every morning.*

The time is now 6:30 A.M. and you're on your way to your 7:00 A.M. to 3:30 P.M. job. You'll work some heavy overtime during the same three months of the year but the rest of the time you're usually home from work by 4:30 or 5:00 P.M. Your honey, on the other hand, doesn't get home from her 8:00 A.M. to 5:00 P.M. job until somewhere between 6:00 and 6:30 P.M. Her goal is to graduate with an MBA so she can advance up the pay scale in her job field. *So three nights a week you make sure dinner is prepared when she gets home from work.* That way she can eat a quick meal before darting off to her 7:00 P.M. class at the local university.

In your spare time, one of the things you love doing together is *renting a few movies and cuddling on the couch to watch them.* However, the one thing she didn't love before you took full responsibility for it was *returning the movies.* After looking at the situation carefully, you realized that returning the movies fits better into your schedule than your sweetheart's.

During the workweek, finding time for the two of you to talk can be tough. So you make it a point to *touch base with her during the day via telephone, voicemail, or e-mail, at least three or four times a week, to see how she is doing.* And you always *let her know you're thinking about her.* Often you'll *ask her if she needs anything. Quite frequently when you need to drop off or pick up your clothes from the dry cleaners, she usually has something to be taken or picked up as well. Because of her busy schedule she finds it difficult to drop off and pick up her clothes from the dry cleaners, so you happily offer to do it for her.* She is very grateful for the time you free up for her. She is so grateful, in fact, she rewards you by spending the time you've saved her on you. Sounds to me like a good trade.

Now in this previous scenario let's look at some examples for how the lists in the workbook might have been used by the man to help him determine the things to do for his woman. Also in the following examples notice that the titles of the sections in the workbook, where the man found key information about his woman, are in quotation marks. Also note how he used his information to determine his everyday actions. You've heard of Eienstein's theory of relativity—$E = mc^2$, right? Well, it has nothing to do with this. Nonetheless, I have a simpler theory of my own, it's ES + PF = AHW. Or,

Engine Style + Proper Fuel = A Happy Woman.

Now this is only an example. Your lady's needs and desires can differ slightly or greatly, depending on her circumstances. Remember that you can benefit tremendously by understanding the relationship between a woman's engine style and its proper fuel. Knowing the right things to do for your sweetheart can reduce and even eliminate the frustration you might have experienced in the past from not having a clue about the right things to do.

Sample of some workbook list areas
From Her "Wish" List

What kind of things can you do to better support her emotionally?	Show a greater interest in her safety and well-being. Protecting her from any situations in which she is fearful.

What he now does for her

 He gets out of bed at 4:00 A.M. to walk his wife to the car when she leaves for the gym. He does it because it's still dark and deserted outside and she is afraid someone could try to abduct her.

From Her "Pet Peeves" and "Hurtful Habits" List

Things that hurt her feelings	When I'm inconsiderate of her or her busy schedule. Not helping her when she needs it most.

What he now does for her

♥ Because she has so little time to get ready for work, he prepares his and her coffee and fixes breakfast for two, every morning.

From Her "Favorites" List

Coffee creamers and sweeteners.	Any brand of flavored fat-free coffee creamer (2 tablespoons). The sweetener in the little blue package (one package).

What he now does for her

♥ He has learned what kind of and how much cream and sweetener to put in her "special" coffee cup.

From "Her Favorites" List

Sentimental things you can say and do that make her feel loved, cherished, and appreciated:	Establish an everyday ritual that is loving. Her very own special coffee mug to use every day. Making her coffee.

What he now does for her

♥ Every morning he washes her special coffee mug, fills it with hot coffee, and with a smile and a kiss he hands it to her.

From Her "Pet Peeves" and "Hurtful Habits" List

Things that hurt her feelings:	When I'm inconsiderate of her or her busy schedule. Not helping her when she needs it most.

What he now does for her

♥ Taking her busy schedule into consideration, three nights a week he prepares dinner ahead of time. When she arrives home from work she can eat a quick healthy meal before she rushes off to her 7:00 P.M. class.

From Her "Not Her Favorites" List

A 🙂		B 🙁
	Returning movie rentals	X

What he does for her now

♥ He takes full responsibility for returning the movies—on time.

From "The Old You" List

When they were dating, he'd call her at least once a day to say

"Hello. I love you" or he'd leave adoring messages on her voicemail,

or e-mail her something nice.

What he does for her now

♥ Again, via e-mail, telephone, or voicemail, he gets in touch with her during their workweek—just to say "Hello" and " I love you."

From Her "Not Her Favorites" List

A 🙂		B 🙁
	Going to the Dry Cleaners	X

What he does for her now

♥ Because she has such a busy schedule, it's difficult for her to drop off and pick up her clothes from the dry cleaners. So he offers to take and pick up her things whenever possible.

In the previous examples, I hope you recognized the helpful kind of information that results from completing the lists in the workbook. In reality, this is only a fraction of the useful data you'll find included in the workbook. There are very few men who, without asking their ladies, could possibly figure out all that stuff. And even for those gentlemen able to figure it out, how would they remember so much information if they didn't write it down? What good would the information do them if they didn't know how to apply it toward pleasing their women?

Let the workbook be your study guide. Study it like you do the newspaper. Occasionally refreshing your memory can help you remember to do the important things almost automatically and get you positive results. Doing the above will increase your skills and help keep them honed for pleasing the woman you love.

A "Surprise" Scenario

Believe it or not, this surprise resulted from a heated discussion I had with my wife and typically enough can't remember what it was about. That just goes to show you how important whatever it was must have been—not very. But apparently at the time it was important or I wouldn't remember so heavily disagreeing with her thoughts on the subject. I'm human too and a stubborn ass every now and then. *But it never takes me long to realize I've been a bad boy, and I need to make things right between me and my wife.*

I remembered she loves to read the newspaper and does so daily. In my desk drawer I have a stack of the comic strip *Love Is* from the classified section of the newspaper. She cuts out the comic strips routinely and only gives them to me if the sentiment is significant to our relationship—and it seems to be much of the time. However, today I'd beat her to the punch. You see, verbal apologies can be so rare, they often have hallucinogenic effects on the recipient. So to make sure she remembers my apology—and the couch will again be a couch—this time I'll surprise her with a very memorable "sorry" and something she loves. That something she loves is reading her newspaper while on the train going to work.

The morning following my blunt blunder, while she was in the shower, *I brought in the newspaper and grabbed the classified section where the* Love Is *comic is located. Then from one of our photo albums I removed a picture of us with our arms lovingly around each other. And* where my wife would have otherwise seen those little chubby exhibitionist lovebirds—streaking as they so often do, there we were, happy again—and fully clothed of course.

I cut the picture to fit perfectly in the space and glued it into place. I reached for a pen to write on a small separate piece of paper my own sentiment to glue over the original one. It read, "Love is, being able to say I'm sorry." Just then I noticed the original sentiment in this particular comic was even more coincidental than my astrological forecast is sometimes, so I used it. It read, "Love is, remembering everyone is entitled to their views."

I put the paper back together and returned it to the driveway where she picks it up every morning while I'm opening the car door for her—she would suspect nothing. After she boarded the train to the city, she'd settle in and start reading her paper. I just waited to get the call, which I did about an hour or so after she left for work. Love is truly full of beautiful surprises and some occasionally sorry ones as well.

A Special-Occasion Scenario

Let's say your sweetheart is very liberated and doesn't care for you to open doors for her or pull out a chair to seat her. Because of her profession, frankly, she doesn't care at all to dine at fancy restaurants. She's a corporate attorney and her long workweek is full of lavish meals with colleagues, clients, and associates—in many of the city's finest restaurants. Always dressed to impress, day in and day out at her job, she is subjected to heavy doses of gentlemanly conduct. Once in a while she'd like to open her own door and pull out her own chair—and longs for a corn dog drenched in mustard.

You've known for quite some time now, one of her favorite pastimes is to spend all day, Saturday or Sunday, in front of the television watching football, eating a bag of cheese puffs. By the third quarter she's beginning to get a little boisterous from all of the cold ones that helped wash it all down. What can you say? So your wife likes to watch football on the weekends while eating a big bag of her favorite snack and throwing back a few beers. How did you get so lucky? *Because she so rarely gets the chance, she would love to go with you to the stadium for a game more than anything else. There she can watch her favorite football team play* and swap those cheese things for a beer-boiled bratwurst heavy on the kraut.

Whatever it might sound like, it's a day in pigskin paradise for her. There's no other place she'd rather be with you than a chaotic football stadium—the complete opposite environment of her posh corporate high-rise office. Is it my imagination or is this scenario sounding too good to be true for many of us? Heck, not if you recognize the fact that for every woman who doesn't care for flowers, candlelight, and hot tubs, there's a man who doesn't care to watch football.

You've been thinking about doing something special for her on a birthday, anniversary, or even Valentine's Day. *You decide to arrange a day together at the stadium, without her knowing.* But to add a more memorable flare—you wisely remember keepsakes and memorabilia are the antioxidants of love. So you decide to *pre-purchase his and her matching jerseys to wear to the game.*

Either you can buy the jerseys with her favorite player's number on the back or you can have the month and day of your particular occasion put on them. For example, 05 on your jersey and 01 on hers would signify your wedding anniversary date of May the 1st. You can use the date of whatever occasion it is you're celebrating at the time. That way when the two of you are standing or sitting together the numbers can represent your anniversary or her birthday. *And don't forget, have your last names and first initials placed on the back of the jerseys.*

You wrap the jerseys nicely in two separate boxes. Then hide the wrapped boxes in the trunk of your car along with an ice chest filled with her favorite snack foods and beverages. (Remember the cheese puffs?) You arrive early at the stadium parking lot so the two you can enjoy your tailgate party and then you can surprise her with the jerseys. To take this event to the next level, you can secretly invite two of your most trustworthy friends to the game. Of course it would be nice of you to offer to pay for their seats. Try to purchase your friend's seats so they'll be sitting across the field from you. Look at the stadium seating chart prior to game day so you know exactly where you buddies will be sitting. And don't forget to bring your binoculars to the game.

In advance, you buy a large roll of white banner paper, the bigger the better. You'll also need to purchase a thick red marker, or paint brush and a can of bright red paint. Then you can write "happy" whatever occasion it is, her name and "I ♥ U" on the banner. (You can find the large rolls of white banner paper, the marker or paint brushes and paint at your local art supply store or hardware store. If you're not into the art thing, try Kinko's or a copying service center in your area. Most copy service centers can make you a large computer-generated banner if that's more convenient for you. Whichever way you choose to complete the banner is fine.) All you need to do now is to get the finished product to your friends so they can bring it to the game. Have your friends hold up the banner at a precise time. However, avoid doing it at the end of a quarter or at half-time because too many fans get up for grub and pub items. And you never know what it might end up saying. When your specific time arrives, let your sweetheart use the binoculars. With a little help from you navigating, you can rest assured she'll remember this special occasion as "The Bomb" forever.

CHAPTER 9

THE ECONOMY ENGINE WOMAN

The Working Woman with Children or the Full-Time Homemaker with Children

This is the most typical style of woman in our society today. She could be a working mom or a stay-at-home mom. Nonetheless she is raising a family. Infants, toddlers, young children, or teenagers, it doesn't matter. For a mother, especially those around the house all day, every day, each stage of having kids comes with its own difficulties and challenges.

I don't agree with the popular old-fashioned notion that full-time homemakers/stay-at-home moms raising children have it made. Their stress is certainly different compared to parents working stressful full-time jobs away from the home, but that in no way means they have it made.

The majority of mothers and fathers working full-time away from the home aren't subject to the occupational hazards of the full-time homemaker raising children. Imagine yourself 12 to 14 hours a day, 7 days a week—an average schedule of a full-time homemaker raising children—and having to cope with the flinging, spitting, crying, screaming, kicking, urinating little cherubs. In many cases it is still expected of you to somehow get the housework done. You also may be judged for the overall quality of your job performance and the ability to continue pleasing your provider.

For the economy engine women, studies have shown a high percentage of them experience drastic fluctuations in their needs and desires, calling for frequent adjustments in priorities. Typically, romance becomes less important than help, appreciation, and understanding. Today, more than anything else from their men, these women want to receive domestic household support, help with the children, and a show of appreciation for their contributions. By now you've probably recognized, the economy engine woman definitely requires a delicate balance—one a man should consider achieving if he wants to keep up the pace and the peace in his relationship race.

If a man works 8 to 10 hours a day and his sweetheart stays home with the kids, it is not one bit unreasonable for her to expect him to take the children off her hands for a while when he returns from work. This doesn't mean that other types of support will no longer be needed such as intimacy, romance, affectionate gestures, and fulfilling her in ways she still expresses a desire for. It simply means he will be doing less of certain things and more of others. It's up to him to find out how her needs have changed and what he can do to accommodate the new. I'm sorry to keep reminding you about the benefits of completing the lists in your workbook, but the answers and solutions to many problem situations and simple ways to prevent them are there for you.

A "Just Because" Scenario

The most likely reasons for people to get up at 4:30 A.M. are to get ready for work or exercise. One of those reasons is true for this man's sweetheart. Monday through Friday she needs to leave the house no later than 6:00 A.M. to get to work on time. Unlike him she is limited to 90 minutes to get ready for work, eat breakfast, and avoid burning her lips and tongue carefully sipping her coffee. As for him, he has "banker's hours." Lucky him you might say. But he still gets up at 4:30 A.M. because that's the time when his family needs and depends on him as a husband and father.

He realizes that because his wife works a full-time job there's no way she could assume full responsibility for him and their nine-year-old daughter—despite what his friends might think. Even if his wife did try to take full responsibility for the breakfasts, sack lunches, dinners, ironing, laundry, grocery shopping, housework, and many other duties that come with having a husband and kids, he couldn't sleep in until 7:00 A.M. every morning; his conscience wouldn't let him.

So he rolls out of bed at 4:30 A.M. and begins his day by sleep-walking his way to the kitchen. First things first: *He starts the coffee. His wife tells him he makes the best coffee she's ever tasted.* While the coffee brews, *he prepares a healthy lunch for his wife. The lunch usually consists of one low-fat yogurt, a whole wheat bagel with peanut butter, a caramel corn or other flavor rice cake, an apple cored and sliced seasoned with lemon and cinnamon, and an English cucumber sliced and seasoned with lemon, chile, and salt.*

Now that his wife's lunch has been made, *he'll prepare another lunch, this time for their nine-year-old daughter.* This is an easy one consisting merely of one peanut butter and jelly sandwich, some grapes or other variety of fruit, chips or crackers, and a juice drink of some sort.

About this time his wife remains a blow-dryer away from being ready to eat breakfast. *He makes breakfast every morning.* The menu looks something like this: a half bagel with something spread over the top like his homemade guacamole with a dash of hot sauce, a jalapeno cheese frittata, or some freshly sliced fruit drizzled with honey and sprinkled with cinnamon. Occasionally, he makes his special peanut butter cinnamon oatmeal. Nonetheless, they always start their day together with a nice breakfast and a freshly brewed cup of coffee.

After breakfast *he helps his wife gather her things for work; then the two of them walkout to the car together. They stand at the car door saying their goodbyes with an arsenal of little kisses (more than 20 seconds' worth) and the first of many "I love yous" for the day. He'll open and close her car door and make his way around to the front of the car where he'll wait for the windshield wipers to remove the thick layer of mist that keeps them from waving goodbye to each other one last time.*

Returning to the house, *it's time to wake up their daughter and prepare her for her day at school.* First, she'll eat her breakfast while he sits with her and sips his second cup of coffee and asks her what she dreamed about in her sleep. When she is finished eating, she will clear the table of her mess and *he will proceed to iron the clothes she'll wear for the day.*

After she's dressed, *he does her hair, which by her request occasionally includes a fancy job of blow-drying and curling her bangs.* She brushes her teeth, grabs her lunch and her backpack, and they're off to school. He likes to walk his daughter to class. If you're a parent, you probably already know that the day will soon come when your child begs you to drop him or her off a mile away from the school to avoid any chance of being seen with you by their friends. So he enjoys it while he still has super-hero status.

Now the time is 7:45 A.M. He's on his way back home to start his workday. He is a real estate professional and enjoys the many conveniences of being able to work from home most of the time. When he gets back to his home office, he'll begin to do the usual marketing, prospecting, and follow-up so vital to succeed in the real estate biz. One of the greatest benefits of working from the home is it enables him to keep certain things around the house in check.

Before he starts working his real estate job, he straightens up the kitchen from the morning's food preparation. Throughout the week he also makes time to do the grocery shopping, pay the bills, balance the checkbook, and when time permits, he prepares a nice sit-down dinner for the family. When his schedule allows it, his goal is to have dinner ready around the same time his wife gets home from work. As often as possible they try to enjoy a nice family gathering at supper time. Honestly, he admits loving to cook and how it quickly became one of his passions, especially when he learned how much his wife admired him for his culinary skills.

After he picks up their daughter from school around 4:30 P.M., they return home and he begins preparing the feast. When his wife gets home from work, it's usually between 5:00 and 6:00 P.M. *Their daughter has completed her homework,* and now they are ready to sit down to another nice home-cooked meal. He'll tell you it's not always easy to do all the things he does in between the phone calls, showing properties, and doing paperwork. But if it weren't for his trusty headset and cordless telephone, he doesn't know if it would all be possible.

After dinner his wonderful wife is kind enough to clean up his culinary aftermath. Their daughter will go take a shower after which she'll get dressed into one of her daddy's oversized T-shirts. *Talking to his little girl through her reflection in the wardrobe closet mirror, he asks her about her day at school while combing the knots from her curly wet hair.*

By this time it's about 7:30 P.M. and time for them to read. Their daughter loves to read to him and his wife. This reading time is considered very special to their daughter. *She reads to one or both of them for around 15 to 30 minutes. Then she brushes her teeth, they tuck her into bed and say their prayers, tell her they love her, kiss her goodnight, and soon she's fast asleep.* He and his wife will then sit together and relax from another productive day on the job for both of them.

Quite often his wife's job can involve an obscene amount of overtime. He won't deny that sometimes she can become completely absorbed by her work; but he doesn't let that stop him from being supportive of her goals. He's more than happy to contribute in any way he can. If it keeps his family happy and healthy, it's worth it to him. To make his wife work harder than she already does by expecting her to look entirely after him, their daughter, and herself, he believes is not characteristic of a man that cares about his wife.

There are no couch potatoes in their home. Everybody wants to contribute whatever, wherever, and whenever they can. Not only has he become an expert at budgeting his time, but he has taken his willingness to pick up the slack (no matter what the slack is) and turned it into a commitment to please his wife—one he is proud of regardless of what it might involve.

He says his wife takes very good care of their daughter and him. They are always receiving compliments from her and being acknowledged with many of the kindest, most thoughtful gestures and praises anyone could receive from a wife and mother. Furthermore, his wife does all the laundry, the heavy house cleaning, and doesn't mind pulling weeds, something he hates. She makes their bed every morning and is almost always ready to mess it up with him again (wink, wink). He and their daughter are always greeted by her with a smile and a kiss, morning, noon, and night. They are always told "I love you" even when there's been a fight. She tells them time and time again, "You can do it, honey, you're so very brave and smart." She never fails to say "thank you" for all he does; she knows it's from his heart.

A "Surprise" Scenario

Friday is fast approaching. However, along with the rest of the full-time homemakers raising children, this guy's wife can't relate to the acronym TGIF nor does she ever really benefit from it. To her, Friday simply means *Saturday, the day he offers to stays home to keep an eye on the kids* is only one day away. Now she can finally do the things she can never seem to accomplish Monday through Friday due to looking after the children. The things his wife needs to get done on Saturdays aren't always fun either. Usually they involve a few errands or the heavier housecleaning duties she can't get done during the week. On occasion *she loves to get her hair and nails done or go out to lunch and take in a movie with a friend.* During the week when he gets home from work, he can tell the two toddlers have worked his wife over pretty good.

So after dinner, which he sometimes volunteers to cook, he'll fill the bathtub, grab the bucket of rubber water toys, and be in hot pursuit of two oblivious little streakers. After he gives them a bath they'll be waiting for him to read them a story and then tuck them into bed. But come Saturday, all day he'll make himself available to entertain and look after the little darlings while his wife does whatever she needs or wants to do for herself and oftentimes for them.

Making himself available to look after the children on Saturdays comes as a great relief to his wife. She appreciates the brief time she gets to spend away from her babies. When she completes her errands, getting her hair and nails done, some heavy housecleaning, or whatever it might be, she, he, and the little ones will spend the rest of day and remainder of the weekend together.

On those Saturdays that his wife gets a manicure, pedicure, and something called "paraffin waxing," he notices she comes home feeling like a new woman. She always tells him how relaxing it is for her to lie back while someone gently works on her feet and hands. Prior to his wife's sharing this information with him, he couldn't imagine a trip to the nail salon being any more invigorating than a haircut.

Listening to his wife carefully has come in handy numerous times. It helps him to recognize when she feels good about something he has done—that way he can do it again. It also helps him recognize when she's gotten to the point where she needs to get away from it all. By that he doesn't mean a trip to Barcelona. *If he remembers correctly—wait a minute, he doesn't have to remember because he knows it for a fact. He wrote it down in his workbook under her favorite ways to relax.* In the past his wife has shared with him how much she loves getting one of those full-on spa treatment deals. He used to be afraid of the term "spa treatment," but only until he discovered that for a fraction of the cost of a European vacation, paradise was a mere 35 minutes away.

His wife had mentioned a place in the little town of Temecula, California, called Glen Ivy Hot Springs Spa. *There for as little as 42 dollars, she could spend the entire day indulging in many included amenities such as swimming pools, saunas, Jacuzzi, steam room, and mud baths. If he was having a great month, for an additional 165 dollars he could treat her to lunch, a couple beverages, 50 minutes of Swedish massage therapy, a pedicure, and a manicure—and don't forget the paraffin wax.* All together, it equals 150 minutes of rejuvenation that without a doubt helps alleviate the tension that sometimes makes her want to put in for her resignation.

Before he secretly made the spa reservation for his wife, he made sure she knew to keep that particular Saturday entirely available. Then he arranged for the kids to spend the entire day and night with the grandparents. Of course his wife asks him what they're doing on that Saturday. He tells her they're going to an all-day business luncheon and seminar his boss arranged and requires his entire sales staff and their spouses attend.

It's now Saturday morning and while his wife drops off the children at Grandma's house, *he quickly packs a tote bag with her sandals, bathing suit, a towel, and some sunscreen. Also, he puts a change of clothes in the bag, her favorite reading material, and the MP3, which he loaded with all her favorite tunes. However, the real jewel is the note he put inside of the bag, on top where she'll be sure to find it. The note expresses his gratitude for her, the wonderful job she is doing with their kids, in their home, and makes her fully aware the children and he couldn't do it without her—the angel watching over them.*

After she reads the note, he is sure she'll be just fine to experience her Saturday spa surprise without him. An entire afternoon of relaxation spent with just herself, peace and quiet, and maybe a few tears of joy when she reads the note he left for her, where he *attached one of their nice family photos.* Maybe she won't be totally alone after all. He believes everybody needs a little time alone. His wife deserves to be pampered and he wishes he could do it this nicely for her more often.

So, now what's he supposed to do while she is pretending to be in Barcelona? That's an easy one. There's an awesome par-69 championship golf course just a few miles down the road and he's going to amorously drive right past it on his way home to begin preparing for a romantic evening with the woman of his dreams—grateful, relaxed, and with incredibly silky smooth legs. Why do you think the kids were sent to the grandparents' house for the entire night?

First he stops at the video store and rents the movie she's been telling him she wants to see so badly. Then it's straight to the market where he buys the items he needs to prepare his wife's favorite salad and dessert for the night's dinner. Having the house clean is another wonderful surprise she'll be sure to enjoy when she arrives back home. Furthermore, not having to deal with two little rambunctious children for the evening perfectly complements the dinner menu, the bottle of her favorite wine, cuddling to a cozy fire, and watching a movie with the man who loves, honors, and appreciates her—and can still prove it.

Because of the intense detail in the scenario that follows, I will not use italicized text. However, at the end of the story there is a checklist to show you everything involved in making the arrangements.

A Special-Occasion Scenario

Only three more months until their fifth wedding anniversary—and what a wonderful five years it's been. The memories of their wedding day and honeymoon can never be forgotten. But sadly, for one reason or another they're slowly beginning to "blend in" to the scenery of family life. During the first couple years of their marriage, he and his wife could still close their eyes and visualize the days when romance and passion reined supreme. But since then they've traded in their quickies in the kitchen for the SUV, three kids, a cockatoo, and karaoke. It's been said "blending in leads to fading out." For him and his wife to let such a memorable time in their lives simply lose its luster and fade away would be a shame.

The passion he possessed for his wife five years ago is still going strong. However, his wife will tell you otherwise, but not in a bad way. You see, the extreme length he went to back then, to create an unforgettable wedding and honeymoon for his wife left her temporarily speechless. So she recognizes his displays of passion and excitement for her were more visible to her in the past, and she knows things can't be that way all the time. The events he secretly arranged for their wedding ceremony eventually brought the reverend to tears too. In fact, the owner of the bed and breakfast inn—where he and his wife stayed on their wedding night and honeymoon—was so intrigued by the groom's plans he wanted to see the decorated room before they vanished for the night.

One day while trying to think of something to do for his wife on their fifth wedding anniversary, he began to daydream about their wedding night and honeymoon. He realizes their fading retrospect will only be rejuvenated by returning to that special place. There she can have a relapse while he rejoices in her favor. Certainly his decision is made.

Over the years many marriage and relationship experts have emphasized the importance of couples finding ways to keep the passion alive. And if a couple is experiencing an unpleasant decrease in the passion between them, the experts suggest finding a way to re-kindle it—and fast. He wants to make sure there isn't any undesirable decrease of passion beginning to take effect in his own marriage. Subsequently he decides for their fifth wedding anniversary he'll set a new standard for ways to rekindle the passion and keep it burning brightly. Here's how he pulls it off.

First he recognizes if he is to recreate their wedding night in a honeymoon suite, it needs to be in the exact same suite they stayed in on that incredible night. In the workbook he has written in his "Romantic History List" all the relevant information he needs to make the occasion almost completely reminiscent of their original experience. Because he has the information from five years ago writ-ten down, arranging the details again isn't any trouble at all. For the last five years of his marriage he has also learned about many new things that are much to his wife's desire.

Most of the things to his wife's liking, he already has written down in his workbook. The workbook helped him not to forget about his wife's love for poetry. He recently discovered the tradition for fifth wedding anniversary gifts is that they're made out of wood. A poem for her written by him and mounted in a frame made of wood sounds like the perfect anniversary gift.

He believes anyone can be a poet. No one should be concerned with what any literary Ph.D. thinks when it comes to love senti-ments. The only thing we should care about is this: when a woman receives anything from the inkwell of a man's heart, moved solely by his vulnerability, she'll consider his prose nothing less than touch-ing. As for the opinions of the hierarchy—their affections he does not seek.

To create his poetic matrimonial memento, he uses his computer, a photograph of him and his wife, and more than a few sessions of covertly scheduled spare time. When the poem is complete, he will have it professionally framed and matted. Wood is being incorpo-rated into the gift in the form of the frame and the paper upon which the poem is written.

Rather than present the gift to her at their anniversary dinner, he decides to do something new and clever. Picking up the phone, he calls information. Then he requests the telephone number to the Four Seasons Biltmore Hotel and Restaurant in Santa Barbara, California. Immediately he asks to speak with the hotel's restaurant manager.

After introducing himself he tells the manager of the wonderful time he and his wife once shared at their fine restaurant. He explains to her that in three months he and his wife will celebrate their fifth wedding anniversary. Then he shares with her how their wedding day was made unbelievably memorable by the restaurant serving the most incredible meal they'd ever had. In addition he boasts how, since becoming Mr. and Mrs., nothing has topped their experience at the Four Seasons restaurant. Finally he shares with the manager his romantic agenda for their upcoming weekend anniversary trip.

When he finishes describing all of the details of the special occasion, the manager is stunned by his desire to please his wife. As a result she expresses an overwhelming desire to accommodate all his needs for the occasion. That's when he asks her to contribute to his plan. She willingly fulfills his request, agreeing to provide him with an actual menu from the restaurant's dining room, offering to send it to him by overnight mail free of charge. He proceeds to schedule their anniversary dinner reservation and thanks the restaurant manager for all of her help. The very next day, the menu arrives in the mail just as the manager promised.

Instead of having the poem framed and matted, he decides to mount it inside of their nostalgic restaurant's dinner menu. He wrote the poem in a menu format, replacing the original menu entrees with loving gestures he would provide her with at a cost of zero dollars $0.00 a pop. On one side of the menu he places the poem. On the other side is a picture of the two of them together.

The day has come and he and his wife have left in the care of those they trust, their kids, the cockatoo, and the...well, so he brought the karaoke machine. As they travel south on Highway 101, his wife only pretends not to know where they're going, at least until they exit Bath Street. Now she knows exactly where they're going. She's very excited to return to the city where so many romantic memories reside. However, she certainly doesn't expect what he secretly has been planning for her over the last few months. For this event I have chosen to show you what was involved in arranging it, by using a checklist.

1. *Destination:*
   ✓ *Santa Barbara, California*

2. *Where they will be staying:*
   ✓ *The Blue Dolphin Inn, Bed and Breakfast*
   ✓ *Three months in advance, he reserved the same room they stayed in on their wedding night*

3. *Anniversary dinner reservations:*
   ✓ *Four Seasons Biltmore Restaurant*
   ✓ *He reserved the same exact table as five years ago*

4. *Special items to be predelivered to the restaurant:*
   ✓ *One bottle of their same favorite wine*
   ✓ *Their wedding dinner wine glasses*
   ✓ *Their custom martini glasses*
   ✓ *One large specially made heart-shaped candle*
   ✓ *A dozen long-stem red roses in a new vase*
   ✓ *Their original dinner place mats that the waitress let them take home as a souvenir from their wedding dinner*
   ✓ *The poem menu*

5. *Prearrangements with the waitress, restaurant manager, and chef, to be done prior to their arrival*
   ✓ *Wine is breathing and on their table*
   ✓ *Their wedding wine glasses are on their table*
   ✓ *Candles are lit and on the table*
   ✓ *Roses on the table, in the vase with water*
   ✓ *Two martinis brought in their glasses after they're seated*
   ✓ *Oysters brought out with the martinis*
   ✓ *One-tier mini anniversary cake for dessert*

6. *Items he will need for their room at the Blue Dolphin Inn*
   ✓ *20 of the same scented candles he originally had in the honeymoon suite, complete with holders*

✔ *Matches*
✔ *The same satin sheets from their wedding night*
✔ *Her favorite bath bubbles and massage oil*
✔ *Favorite wine, opener, and glasses*
✔ *Ninety minutes of the music they both love*
✔ *One cassette/CD player*
✔ *Eight dozen red rose petals for the bed, tub, floor, and staircase leading up to their room*
✔ *Wedding memorabilia*

In she rides on a tidal wave of deja vu. She comes to rest on the shore of reminiscence. After a proposed toast, the martinis, and the oysters, they are now ready to order the main course. A conspiring waitress slowly approaches the table and enviously yet kindly hands his wife the menu of her lifetime. But as you know, dinner is only the beginning of the surprises he has prepared for her. His wife still humorously recalls how upon returning from their wonderful flashback dinner, he convinced her his intestinal tract was behaving rather violently. "It must have been something I ate," he told her. Then he begged her to please give him a few minutes for what he had since assured her wasn't going to be quiet time.

So his wife wisely chose to wait in the main house. The innkeepers did just as they agreed to do earlier—hold her hostage until he returned for her. Sometimes to get the job done it may require some pretty strange and on occasion temporarily embarrassing tactics. But in the end everybody is laughing and happy as can be. So, while his wife thought he was busy reading the newspaper, he was instead on his way to set up their room completely reminiscent of the first wedding night they spent together.

Hauling his bag of tricks from the trunk of their rental car, up the stairs to their suite, he begins to unpack it and arrange the room exactly the way it was on that memorable night. While the Jacuzzi tub is filling with hot water and bubbles, he carefully lights 20 scented candles, then strategically places them around the room. Next he begins playing the CD of their favorite wedding songs. He spreads the rose petals all over the bed, which he has since remade with the satin sheets from their wedding night. He fills their special wine glasses with their most sentimental wine. Finally upon exiting the room, using the remainder of the rose petals, he covers the top of the tub, the bedroom floor, and the entire staircase leading up to this suite retreat. This time she'll have to agree, it really does smell like roses.

CHAPTER 10

THE HIGH-PERFORMANCE ENGINE WOMAN

The Full-Time Homemaker Without Children or Whose Children Have Grown and Gone

This is the third and final engine style of women, and could be considered somewhat rare these days. When a gentleman's lady has this style engine, the most important thing he can focus on is her, her, her, and more of her. Unlike the men involved with women in one of the other two engine styles, men involved with women in this chapter don't need to be as domestically diverse. That's because the high-performance engine woman has never had or no longer has children to look after, doesn't need to or choose to report to a job, tends to experience much less stress, and probably has a lot more free time.

But don't make the foolish mistake of thinking these women are living a life of leisure. There are many highly educated and financially secure wives who choose not to work or have children, or their kids have already left home. Nevertheless, these ladies can be very active as volunteers and contribute a great deal to their communities and elsewhere while still keeping a good house and home. Therefore, nothing shy of having a great deal of respect for these ladies shall be allowed. (Thanks to my dear friend Marilyn Ross for enlightening me further in this area!)

Because of the absence of children in these relationships, the attention of the man can stay focused 100 percent on his sweetheart. Once again he is advised to always express his interest in her and in the things she does throughout her day. In addition to that she will fare beautifully when provided with his undivided attention, admiration, loving support, and affections and desires for her expressed regularly. There are two specific things he can do to help her avoid feeling lonely or inadequate:

1. Encourage her hobbies, pastimes, or volunteer work.
2. Involve her and include her in his thoughts and daily routine as much as possible.

Learning to be a domestic diplomat and never ruling out a good trade is always a smart idea. For example, some men love to cook while some women love to work up a sweat tending to the yard. Not to encourage conspirators but sometimes after a man tastes his honey's cooking, he might well prefer to develop his culinary skills. And a woman might choose to pursue courses in the plumbing and electrical trades to protect herself from becoming a widow prematurely. If you can make a souffle and she can mow and blow, I say, more power to ya. It's a great idea to remain flexible when it comes to swapping domestic roles and duties; it could function as superglue in the bond of your relationship.

Before we get started with the scenarios in this chapter, imagine yourself being the high-performance engine woman. Picture this: The man in your life depends 100 percent on you to fulfill his needs and desires and take care of the household. Meanwhile, you're thinking about going back for your master's degree and volunteering 40 hours a week at the senior center. If you applied yourself correctly, do you think by cooking meal after meal, cleaning the house, and doing your best to take care of your man, you'd be happy without any emotional support or appreciation from him?

If you were not recognized by your man (remember you're pretending to be the woman here) for your diligent efforts to care for him and the household, would you feel good about continuing in your role? I'm sure you're no different from most of the population in that you, too, don't like being taken for granted. You'd want to know you were appreciated. You would want to be shown by your man on a regular basis how much he appreciated and valued everything you did, including your contributions to the public. You'd feel good about things and be motivated to continue doing your best. Nevertheless, you could still use an occasional break from it all. And with that we'll begin this chapter's scenarios.

A Just-Because Scenario

He wakes to the overwhelmingly pleasant smell of his sweetheart's baking. And he'll tell you these are no ordinary baked goods. Extreme pride and care go into everything she makes. Biscuits, scones, croissants—you name it and she makes them all taste great. She serves them with one of his favorite breakfast entrees chosen because she knows it's one of his favorites. For years he hasn't needed his alarm clock to wake him; the delicious smells coming from the kitchen are enough.

After he's up and showered, he throws on a t-shirt and shorts, then heads out into the kitchen. There she is, the most wonderful woman in the world, serving up his breakfast again.

Many experts say a person's mood for the entire day can be heavily influenced by what they say, feel, and do in the first moments after they wake in the morning. In other words, it can be difficult to have a good day when it begins by jamming your little toe into the foot of an iron-post bed on a cold winter morning.

He since found the best time to say something nice to his honey is definitely in the morning, and by doing so, coincidentally makes it easier for him to say more nice things to her throughout the rest of the day.

Since confirming this belief of saying and doing something nice to start the day off on the right foot, *he never lets a morning pass without telling his honey something sweet. For example, when he greets her good morning he says, "Good morning, honey. I love you."* And that starts the day quite nicely. *Furthermore, to show her how much he ap-*

preciates her taking such good care of him, *every morning he greets her with a smile, a kiss, and a warm hug.* When they sit down to eat, she loves for him *to say things like, "It smells delicious," "This tastes great," "You've done it again," "It gets better every time,"* and the most important one of all, *"Thank you for breakfast, honey."*

Saying *"please"* and *"thank you"* should be the first important and most sought after lessons parents relentlessly attempt to teach their children. How can any of us not remember being asked by our parents, "Now what do you say?" Unfortunately, as adults, please and thank you have for many become the most taken for granted and unused words in the English language, right up there with "I love you."

After they finish eating breakfast, *he helps her clear off the table and thanks her again for another wonderful breakfast. Before he leaves for work, he always gives her a hug and kiss by the door. Then he tells her to have a nice day and that he loves her—yes, again.*

Throughout his workday when he gets a little break—and there is always a little break—he'll call his wife just to say, "Hello." He also knows how much she loves it when he tells her he misses her and is thinking about her. When she tells him what she's making for dinner that night *he'll say something like, "I can't wait to taste it," "I love everything you make," or "You're such a fabulous cook,"* and *"I'm so lucky to have you." It often makes her day to hear him say things like that. He encourages her hobbies, pastimes, and volunteer work. He inquires about them regularly and likes to know how her current projects are going. She has many talents. And he makes it a point to always tell her she can be the greatest at whatever she chooses to do.*

Four times a month he arranges to meet her at a restaurant or his office for lunch. Occasionally, at lunchtime, he'll meet her at home and skip the meal entirely. Together they will burn about 700 (quickie) calories. Now there's a diet that works! Once or twice a week and depending on the finances, he offers to take his hardworking woman out for dinner. It doesn't have to be somewhere expensive, just as long as she's relieved of the cooking every now and then. He enjoys cooking a little himself, so periodically he volunteers to cook dinner for her. But her favorite is definitely when they cook together. Music, wine, a little pasta with shellfish in a cream sauce, asparagus, some candlelight, and just like a great Portu-guese chef would say, "Bam!"

Most evenings will find them home together. However, they encourage each other to have their own time to see dear friends and family, engage in their favorite pastime, or just read a book. They definitely don't abuse their guy's or girl's night out privilege. But good friends and family always come in handy so they should be spent time with occasionally. He encourages her to stay in touch with dear friends and family by engaging in respectful social events and activities whenever she feels the need. Happily she extends the same consideration to him. Before they doze off for the night, *he likes to say a little prayer—aloud so she can hear—and in the prayer, he thanks God for blessing him with a most angelic woman and his willful desire to remain a good man.*

A Surprise Scenario

Five days a week he gets dressed in one of his many freshly dry-cleaned and pressed suits. His sweetheart sees to it his suits are taken and picked up from the cleaners once a week. From the beginning he has emphasized how important it is that she check all his shirts, coats, and pants pockets prior to her lugging the massive pile of silk, wool, and cotton to the cleaners.

He assures her that thoroughly checking his pockets is not a self-righteous attempt to prove himself to her. He is simply setting her up to unknowingly find the things he will purposely place in his pockets for her to discover. In the past he's left simple little notes that say things like "Thank you for keeping me clean and pampered, I love you," or " Honey, you are the only woman in the world who suits me; I love you." The cornier the better. On occasion she would find a gift certificate for getting her nails done or a prepaid facial appointment card. Sometimes she could even find lunch or dinner date offers at one of her favorite restaurants.

Once he left two bags of her favorite tea in one of his coat pockets. Attached to the bags was a note that read, "Have a tea on me, but don't wait. Find this hot pot that whistles our theme. From then on it shall sing. With each day comes but a new song. To keep you warm inside and out, in a beautiful way, and our whole life long."

Drinking hot tea in the evenings is one of his darling's favorite pleasures. For them, drinking tea together brings back very romantic memories from the years gone by. From this ancient tradition and one of its methods of preparation, he created their first family heirloom. His beloved mate can now boil the water for her tea in a kettle that whistles words of love.

Because he wants her to find the tea bags with note/clue, and then find the teakettle, he'll wait until the same morning she always takes his suits to the cleaners to plant the pocket bait. Then on that morning, when she isn't anywhere near the kitchen, he'll take the old teakettle out from inside the oven, where she puts it every night after her cup of tea, and replace it with the new one. Before he leaves for work, he'll slip the tea bags with note/clue into one of his dirty suit's pockets. *By the way, this is not just an average teakettle. He personally wrote a poem for her and had the poem, his name, "I love you" and the date all engraved on the new kettle.*

When she finds the tea bags and note/clue in his coat pocket, she'll definitely be able to find her surprise. When she does find the kettle, hot tea won't be the only thing brewing in their home.

Surprise Scenario

You and your honey are waiting for escrow to close on your very first home. The home was already vacant at the time your offer was accepted. On the day you received the keys, you can still recall that very same morning when you both agreed dinner at your favorite restaurant was a great way to celebrate the occasion. Unfortunately, by afternoon it was raining heavily and the restaurant you and she love most was too far away for the current weather conditions. Just then you have an idea.

You can surprise your wife by preparing dinner for her in your new home; you'll just have to keep it simple. Suddenly you realize the home is not even equipped with the simple items needed to prepare a meal of any kind. As a matter of fact there isn't even a place to sit. It seems to me as though this opportunity is becoming more attractive by the minute. Secretly you arrange this romantic engagement and first-ever meal together in your new home. Again you depend on and refer to your workbook and its lists to help you create the event.

Your preparation begins by deciding which foods will be on the evening's menu, none of which need to be cooked. *Aside from a few necessities such as a makeshift table, candles, matches, radio, ice chest, a large blanket to sit on, glassware, silverware, and napkins, everything else you can find in your workbook.*

Below, you'll find the list of items used to create this occasion.

1. Dinner:
   - ✓ *Three types of her favorite cheeses*
   - ✓ *Two types of her favorite deli meats*
   - ✓ *Three types of her favorite fruits*
   - ✓ *Two types of her favorite crackers*

2. Beverage:
   - ✓ *One bottle of her favorite wine with opener*

3. Ambiance:
   - ✓ *20 candles placed around the room*
   - ✓ *Matches*
   - ✓ *One single long-stem red rose*
   - ✓ *Flower vase with water*

4. Music:
   - ✓ *Her favorite Spanish guitar artist*
   - ✓ *Radio or CD player*

5. Dessert:
   - ✓ *Chocolate-covered strawberries*

6. The location of the meal:
   - ✓ *You set your table in the middle of the master bedroom, which your list indicated as her favorite room in a home*

You make arrangements to pick her up after you get out of work and run a few errands, while in fact you really use the "errand time" to deliver your portable bistro. Making your wife believe that the two of you will still celebrate somewhere local because of the rain, she waits for you to return home. When you pick her up, she is so excited about the house she asks if you'll drive her by before going to dinner, just as you predicted she would. You willingly oblige her. Just then the rain begins to pour out of the sky torrentially (not done by you). You and your honey pull into the driveway of your new home. So that you can enter the home without her, you insist she wait while you go inside to open the garage door and pull in the car so she won't get soaked. While she waits in the car, you enter the house and head straight for your temporary dining room. Quickly you proceed to set the table with the food, pour the wine, and light the candles. Returning to the car, you pretend to be very distraught and inform her that someone has broken in and horribly vandalized the home. Almost brought to tears, she insists on seeing the damage, after you answered, "Yes, honey, the police are on their way." You take her by the hand and enter the house together. You've made sure to shut the master bedroom door before you brought her in the house.

Now guiding her slowly down the dark hallway, you prepare her to witness the worst of the damage that has occurred in her favorite room of the house. She opens the door to the master suite and finds the only thing vandalized is her own gullibility. After she socks you on the arm a few times, she is more than astonished and flattered by what you prepared for her. How will she ever be able to move away from that house?

A Special Occasion Scenario

He stopped collecting baseball cards when he graduated high school. He got tired and frustrated from reading the price guides with inflated, misleading value descriptions. They had falsely led him to believe—and one time too many—his cards were worth such prices or at least somewhere near what he would need for the down payment on a new car. However, his last trip to the plate was with his most prized baseball card of the lot. For sure he thought this card, with one of the legendary home run "kings" pictured on it, would bring him that much closer to his new wheels.

Ten years later he finally got his wheels, no thanks to Hank Aaron. He also got married to a very nice woman. The two had dated each other for approximately two years when they decided to wed. Now it seems as though his past experience with collecting baseball cards wasn't a complete waste of his time after all. Even though he never came anywhere near recouping his overall investment, still he learned a valuable lesson. Collecting baseball cards taught him how to recognize when something was valuable enough to keep. It also proved that good card collectors and traders know and study the game, the teams, the players, major leagues, minor leagues, and even college sometimes. Over time he realized every card in his collection was in one way or another desirable and to some degree valuable.

One card all by itself might have seemed worthless to him, while the same card to one of his trading buddies or collectors, was highly desirable and sought after. So you see, from collecting and trading these bubble gum–scented heros, all along without his even knowing, he was acquiring skills. Later in life those skills would enable him to sharply pay attention to detail while at the same time recognizing value—not so much for the financial benefits, but for the emotional interests of another person, the woman he loves.

Throughout the years he and his wife have spent together, they've done quite a few things, including some local traveling within their state. Regardless of what they would do or where they would go, he treated each trip, event, and special occasion with the same enthusiasm and watchful eyes as when he opened a pack of baseball cards as a child—immediately he could recognize a keeper for his own collection and sometimes another's. In the case of his wife and him and their life spent together up to this point, *all along he has recognized and collected love memorabilia.*

He had things like ticket stubs from their first movie, play, and concert together. Pictures and brochures of memorable trips and special occasions have also been hot on his list of save-worthy items. From pressed dried flowers, a coffee cup saucer with heart-shaped coffee stain, even chopsticks from an unforgettable honeymoon sushi dinner, anything can be saved. No one can minimize the value of these kinds of collectibles. With each year that passes, no matter what condition love collectibles are in, they continue to increase in sentimental value.

Just like the ballplayer statistics, batting average, home runs, bases stolen, or a pitcher's earned run average, he knew when something was worth keeping. After just a few years of marriage he collected more memories than he ever had baseball cards. Valentine's Day was only a few months away now and he *came up with a great gift alternative to roses, truffles, and teddies (maybe not all teddies)*.

So this year his wife's Valentine's Day gift *will be an assortment of romantic things he has collected along with some perfect timing. He'll begin with a book of memorabilia from their life together so far.* From enough items collected to fill a modest-sized collector's case, in his spare time he sorted through them all. Piece by piece, no matter what the item was, it had its place in their history. *By using his computer, a copier, some cutting and pasting, he organized the contents of the book. The result of his and his wife's unpublished past was a beautiful scrapbook of their most romantic and sentimental trips and occasions, all chronologically arranged and with a wonderfully happy picture of him and her together on the cover.* This was one the best coffee-table books he had ever seen.

Some time ago his wife mentioned something to him about a wristwatch. One day while visiting a shopping mall with her, she tried it on in front of him. Now he knew exactly which watch she would eventually like to have. By documenting the watch information on her wish list in his workbook, he can make the right purchase.

Whenever he has one or two gifts to give to his wife, he tries his hardest to avoid the conventional use of boxes and gift wrap. So instead he plans with the manager of a major well-known bookstore a few miles from their home, a much more memorable way for his Valentine to receive the book.

After work he drives straight to the bookstore and immediately phones his wife to tell her the traffic is awful so he's going to be home later than usual. Furthermore, he tells her because he's running behind schedule, and if they want to be on time to their dinner reservation he needs her to run an errand for him before he gets home. He and the manager of the bookstore have since found a location on the shelves to place the book. The errand he gave his wife to run was for her to go to the bookstore and pick up the last copy of a first edition book going out of print.

The key to this plan's success was having the full cooperation of the bookstore manager. He told his wife he had already spoken with the bookstore manager and he would have the book waiting behind the counter for her. About 15 minutes after he spoke with his wife on the telephone, she arrived at the bookstore. She did exactly as he advised. She found the bookstore manager, then explained why she was there. But he pretended to have forgotten all about pulling the last book from the shelf to put it behind the counter. As she and the manager head toward this very special book, he follows them carefully, so she won't see him. Bless the manager's heart, he was having a very good time pretending the book she was sent to get was, in fact, sold out.

Just then, "Wait just a minute. Do I know you?" the manger asked. And before she could even answer, "You know, you look very familiar to me. I just know I've seen you somewhere recently," he continued. By this time his wife looks to be getting disturbed. Before she starts to walk out the manager glides over to the shelf and pulls the book from it. "Now I know where I've seen you before!" he shouts. He finally hands her the book and with one last attempt to refrain from laughing, he says, "Are you gonna try and tell me this is not you on the cover and the handsome young gentleman standing right over there isn't your husband?"

The tears began to fall as soon as he wished her a happy Valentine's Day. As if she needed to be shocked again, he still had the watch to give her. However, presenting the watch to her would be much easier. After they drove back to the house and dropped off her car and the book, they immediately left for dinner. He purposely made their dinner reservation for later in the evening to allow for the time needed at the bookstore.

When they arrive at the restaurant, and only after they are seated, he excuses himself to the men's room. He actually goes to talk to the hostess, who he had spoken with earlier that day. She had agreed to wear his wife's soon-to-be-gift watch until they were finished eating their dinner. For dessert the hostess would casually deliver to their table, a decadent chocolate masterpiece. They ask the hostess if she's having a nice Valentine's Day. Then she shares with them the beautiful watch her boyfriend bought for her as this year's gift. Meanwhile, he begins to wonder if his wife would've rather received a wristwatch instead of a memory book. Na. This year he thinks she'll be just fine to get them both.

His wife is happily sharing in the hostess' excitement, maybe even a bit enviously and then before you know it, the hostess is putting the watch on his wife's wrist. "Go ahead try it on, see how it looks and feels on you. And by the way, get used to it," the hostess said as she turned and walked away from their table. The only thing he could say to explain was, "Honey, what time is it—on your new watch? Happy Valentine's Day."

That was the last of all the scenarios and the final engine style of women. Don't forget my intentions for the *italic* text throughout the last three chapters on the engine styles of women. Notice how all of the things done for the woman in each just-because scenario was specifically meant to provide *daily* domestic help, appreciation, support, and recognition in those areas particularly where the woman needed it most—according to her certain circumstances.

I used italic text to make it clearer for you to notice the specific types of things being done in each scenario. If you so choose, you can also consider doing the same things or similar ones for your sweetheart. But before you begin to do anything for her, remember first to take into account which one of the three engine styles she's running. The reason for this is that there is one exception you'll always want to consider before you choose the ways in which you'll begin to provide for her. The exception applies to the just-because scenarios and the domestic duties being done throughout them.

For example, if your honey is a high-performance engine woman, don't use the just-because scenario and approach for the economy engine woman to get ideas on how to please your lady. Because if your honey is a high-performance engine woman, you shouldn't have to leave work early all the time to stop and buy the weekly groceries. Equally unnecessary would be for you to always have to take and pick up your suits from the cleaners. So when it comes to domestic duties and the just-because scenarios, stick to the chapter that is relative to your mate's engine style.

It's also important you find out in which specific areas your partner needs your help, appreciation, and recognition the most before you start doing, providing, and saying the wrong things. That's why I emphasize so much the importance of completing the workbook. Once you determine what your woman's engine style is you can better understand that style and learn to use the information in your workbook to always stay considerate of her needs and desires.

As far as the surprise and special occasion scenarios are concerned, they tend to be based more on giving tangibly, creatively, and sentimentally—not so much domestically. Subsequently, some of the concepts and ideas shared with you in the surprise and special occasion scenarios are a bit more universal and could be used for all three engine styles of women. So no matter which style you find under the hood of your honey, you can use any of the ideas from the surprise and special occasion scenarios to give your woman's heart a nice kick start. Not necessarily in the exact way they are done in the book, but by referring to your lists in the workbook you'll be able to plug in specific items that are to your mate's liking.

When in doubt, double-check your workbook lists. You can't say the wrong thing or come across in the wrong way to a list—and best of all you can't hurt its feelings.

CHAPTER 11

POLE POSITION

Requalifying for the Big Race

In this chapter you'll learn a lot of easy things you can do for your significant other, many of which may even sound "familiar" to you. I say familiar because, if you think back for a moment, back to the beginning of the relationship with your mate, you'll know exactly what I'm talking about. And I bet you'll recall your undaunted efforts to "qualify for the big race." If you're like a lot of men, more than likely you'll remember doing many of these familiar things for your woman back then. Each and every one had a profound positive affect on her. If you continue to do them regularly, they have the ability to keep your sweetheart happy for a lifetime. A man's commitment to continue giving in a few or all of these ways often results in his relationship heading for victory lane.

Women have a great deal of respect for a man who is considerate of their needs and desires emotionally, spiritually, physically, and materialistically. In the beginning of a relationship, men are often very attentive in all the areas I've mentioned. However, a lot of women will admit after a few years—less in many cases—of marriage or an exclusive relationship, things tend to change radically. The reality is this: Things don't have to change, but we let them.

From the days of old, treating a woman like a lady has changed in many ways. It's not just pulling out chairs, opening doors, or providing chocolate and roses that keeps women happy. Nevertheless, most women would be pleased if the men in their lives made even the slightest attempt to be considerate in the ways I'll share with you throughout this chapter. In fact, you probably did many of these things automatically and did them very well while attempting to secure "pole position" in the beginning of your relationship.

Just in case you've forgotten what an attentive debonair gentleman you may have been, in the workbook there's a list called "The Old You" list. This is for the lady in your life to complete because she is sure to know what she loved so much about you in the beginning of the relationship that has since vanished (aside from your waist line and hair). It won't hurt matters to treat your sweetheart as you did in the beginning—when she fell in love with you. Anything you can remember doing for her, or she says you used to do and she grew to love you for, do for her again and continue to—until death do you part. Remember, you haven't won this race yet. And whatever you do, don't say, "She stopped doing this and that first." The tit-for-tat attitude will get you absolutely nowhere—except maybe divorced.

We men should aim to teach and bear burdens with patience, kindness, and love. Teaching our ladies and children through examples set by our own behavior—no matter how difficult it seems—is always the responsibility of a true leader in any worthy cause. We must also be able to humble ourselves and be willing to make sacrifices—and we can do so without losing our dignity.

Give Back What You Gave to Get Her in the Beginning

♥ Hold her hand when you're out with her.

♥ Always open doors for her.

♥ Pull out her chair at restaurants, dinner parties, and anywhere in public.

♥ Ask if she would like you to butter her bread (some women really eat that one up).

♥ Gas up the car for her.

♥ Put on her coat and remove it for her.

♥ Sit close to her whenever possible.

♥ Always offer to carry bags or heavy items.

♥ Walk her to her car when she leaves for work or the gym.

♥ Always greet her with a hug and kiss when she returns home, and the same when she's leaving to go somewhere.

♥ Continue, or begin, using a pet name for her, e.g., honey, sweetheart, babe (creates a positive affirmation).

♥ Kiss and hug her goodbye whenever you leave somewhere without her.

♥ Kiss her good morning—after brushing, of course.

♥ Kiss her first thing when you get home from work.

♥ Kiss her good night, every night.

♥ Kiss her in public and not with your tongue either; soft gentle little kisses on the lips or a quick pass by her neck or ear if you have a booth.

♥ Hug her daily, many times with a 30-second minimum.

♥ Kiss her daily, softly for 20 seconds.

♥ Tell her you love her at least twice a day, morning and before bed—more is better.

♥ Tell her she looks beautiful every chance you get, especially without makeup, she'll think you've lost it completely, but man, she'll really soak it up when you're not looking.

♥ Tell her she's got a beautiful body and you love her just the way she is.

♥ Tell her how lucky a man you are to have a woman like her.

♥ Tell her you missed her or are missing her, every day if possible.

♥ Call her at work just to say, "Hello," "I love you," or "I just wanted to hear your beautiful voice" (only if she won't get in trouble from her boss).

♥ Leave loving messages on her cell phone voicemail in your best Barry White voice.

♥ If the two of you have a special song together occasionally leave as much of it on her voicemail as possible.

♥ Send her e-mails, virtual kisses, and greeting cards whenever you have a chance, or simply write something sweet—"You're looking e-licious today."

♥ Always say "please" when you ask her for something and "thank you" when she does anything for you.

♥ If your significant other cooks, tell her she is the greatest and always say "this is delicious" after the first bite, even if it's not that great.

♥ Leave her little notes in surprise places—her purse, her lunch box, the speedometer in her car. Or turn your weaknesses into strengths. For instance, if you not going to replace the empty toilet paper roll at least write something nice on it like, "Just stinking of you." No! Just kidding. Try this, "Don't ever change, I love you!"

♥ If you're a slob, like so many of us tend to be, and you leave anything and everything for your partner to pick up, pick up after yourself! You'll be surprised at the appreciation you can receive from that gesture alone. If you haven't the desire to make things any easier for your super woman, then for crying out loud don't make 'em more difficult for her.

This next list contains what could be considered some of the obvious and not so obvious events and beneficial times throughout our everyday lives where we could choose to do something special for our women.

1. Birthdays
2. Anniversaries, yearly, monthly, or your first date
3. Valentine's Day
4. Christmas
5. Mother's Day
6. New job
7. Job promotion
8. Working a lot of overtime

9. Pregnant
10. Gave birth
11. Graduation
12. Just because
13. Engagement proposal
14. Wedding day
15. Honeymoon
16. Moving to a new home
17. Special achievements, losing weight, finishing a project, passing a big test
18. Returning home from a trip
19. Surgery or hospitalization
20. Home, sick in bed
21. Every day
22. Retirement

Any of the previous 22 occasions can be made into unforgettable moments if you choose. Many of them are scattered throughout the year and a few of them only occur once or twice in a lifetime. However, number 21, "every day," is by far the best. You don't have to always do something elaborate, just something to remind her just how much she is loved and appreciated by you. Occasionally you can show her how special she is to you by doing something outrageous. Some people may think you are going overboard, but I believe it is just the kind of thing that is lacking in most marriages and relationships today.

The following is a list of some prime times when you should tell the woman that you love "thank you." She should never go without being recognized for doing these things, you should not either if you're doing them. Never underestimate the emotionally medicinal power and effectiveness of simply saying "thank you."

1. Cooking meals
2. Doing the dishes
3. Cleaning the house
4. Doing you any favors
5. Doing the laundry
6. Ironing

7. Taking and picking up the kids (school, practices, lessons, wherever)
8. Taking care of the kids
9. Helping the kids with homework or school projects
10. Doing the grocery shopping
11. Fixing things around the house
12. Washing the cars
13. Mowing the lawn
14. Pulling weeds
15. Planting flowers or new plants
16. Preparing for the entertaining of family or friends at your home
17. Bringing you something to eat or drink
18. Putting things away around the house
19. Picking up after you and the kids

All of the nice things being mentioned in this chapter are vital for long-term happiness in any relationship. The reasons for and the benefits of doing the things recommended in this chapter might be better understood if you imagine them as game strategies to decrease your odds of losing. Look through the eyes of the players on any professional sports team. The players analyze their opponent before, during, and after the game to improve their chances of victory with every season that passes.

But in our case it's not a normal length season and the game being played is a different one. Let's call it the Resentment Game. It is played every day of the year and its season has no end. If we neglect our teammate, she will likely become resentful. Many times this resentment can build slowly and silently. Then right before our very own eyes our once passionate teammate has suddenly become our opponent. Looking at the increasing number of people getting divorced every year, you'll find the vast majority of them didn't keep their heads in the game.

Now envision the scene in just about every football or boxing film. The players and coaches are gathered around some old movie projector—to watch film. There is no popcorn, no hot dogs, no candy or soda. The determined players and coaches feed only on the desire to learn, analyze, discuss, and document their opponent's weaknesses and strengths. They even go so far as to watch themselves. They critique their own performance and acknowledge any areas in particular where they need improvement.

This strategic technique the professional athletic teams have been using all along must pay off somehow. It must further improve their chances of winning, or they wouldn't be wasting their time. This same strategy can also be used similarly in a marriage or relationship. Although our goals, in more ways than one, will be a little bit different from those of the professional athlete.

First and foremost, we're not searching for flaws in our significant other. We're searching for ways to keep them enthusiastic and make sure their love for the game remains passionate and steadfast. Second, some good reasons for us to complete the workbook are so we can learn and study the information that pertains to our significant other. The reason we choose to improve our knowledge is not so we can defeat our teammate, but to defeat the possibility of our teammate ever becoming our rivalrous opponent. Third, this workbook is similar to the film projector. Use it to keep yourself up-to-date with the strategies you'll need to win her heart over and continue winning it over season after season.

"There is no sweeter victory than the victory of love. Ask anyone who has possessed it for any length of time and lost it unwillingly."

—Steven A. Guerrero

CHAPTER 12

SOUL FUEL AND FAST-TRACK FOOD

The Easy No-Cook Breakfast, Lunch, Dinner, and Dessert Menu With a Side Order of Sentimental Word Ideas to Keep Your Honey's Heart and Soul Happy

A lot of men experience some level of difficulty—mostly severe—when they attempt to express loving feelings to their beloved ladies. Furthermore, most men believe they are incapable of conveying the love they feel for someone by putting it into written words. For every man who neglects to impart kind and loving words, both verbal and written, there is a woman who suffers greatly. Many men don't realize or believe there are immeasurable rewards that occur from occasionally giving a simple greeting card or poem possessing a few endearing words.

However, if you believe like a lot of men do, that some scholastic credential or gifted talent is needed to write poetry or thoughtful sentiments you've got it all wrong. One need not be an accomplished writer to shower a woman with beautifully written sentimental keepsakes on a regular basis.

A few minutes spent on the greeting card aisle at the local supermarket is all a man should need to find a card that will convey how he feels about his honey. There are even more resources of unlimited variety on the Internet. On the web you can obtain everything from

115

custom cards and poems to personally written love letters. You can even have a mini-novel written about you and your lover's life together. Almost anything you believe you can't do yourself or you don't have the time to do, the web can connect you with someone who will happily and professionally provide the service—for a fee, of course.

Take a little time to notice and you'll soon find there is more to life online than trading, bootlegging, and chatting. In the Fuel Sources section at the back of the book, I've listed some Internet sites that will blow you away with the items and services they provide. If you like, you can also visit my website www.StartHerHeart. com. There you can find links for many creative sites that offer the services I mentioned above plus more. You'll be hooked once you've seen how easy it really can be to provide your sweetheart with thoughtful and romantic gifts of all types.

The reality is if you express your loving feelings for a woman in writing of any kind, poetic or not, the outcome is totally in your favor. When you give her a greeting card, poem, note, or anything with a heartfelt sentiment written on it, like with most women, her feelings won't be hurt if you didn't write it yourself. Because to her as long as you chose it, it must mean you have those feelings for her—and she's touched.

Although I must admit if you do have the slightest ability to express in your own written words, the feelings you have for your woman, you are in possession of a very powerful love tool. I've yet to meet a woman who doesn't deeply cherish the loving words her man has written for her (no matter how cheesy). Therefore, any loving words you provide for your honey, cheddar or Swiss, will be greatly appreciated by her. In the end, whether the words are yours or the prose of another, they can inspire her spirits and fill her heart with joy. Here are some ideas for how you can provide, in writing, many different things which will convey to a woman the deep love and appreciation you have for her. All these items are available to you and are easily found in many retail stores, supermarkets, shopping malls, bookstores, on the Internet, inside of your home, and believe it or not, some of the most heartwarming sentiments pertaining to love can be found in the Bible.

You can find most of the following items with nicely written sentiments already on them. And all of them, if you're able, can be custom created by using your own written words to express your feelings of love and gratitude for the woman you love.

♥ Greeting cards, made custom or store bought. If you have a home computer, purchase a greeting card software program. You can really get personal by creating cards using scanned pictures of you and your sweetheart and children.

♥ Poetry. Don't be afraid to try. Even if you sound like Dr. Seuss, believe me she probably won't give a damn, Sam I am.

♥ Lyrics from her favorite love songs. You can occasionally use a familiar song line or two and mix them in with the other text you write. She will find it charming of you that you know her favorite songs.

♥ Daily devotional booklets. You can find many of these type books in the romance and self-help sections of any bookstore, drugstore, supermarket, or card shop.

♥ Wall plaques or framed poems. Most gift shops and some florists carry items like this. And don't forget to first check on the Internet.

♥ Poems, engraved on silver, copper, or stainless steel plates, pots, pans, glassware, and even teakettles. (Remember?) This can be pricey, but it's well worth its weight in gold and lasts forever.

♥ Scriptures from the Bible. I can guarantee you'll find the most beautiful examples of what it truly means to give love freely and passionately—eloquently written and reinforcing the commitment God intended for us to keep so our marriages would remain strong, rewarding, and monogamous.

♥ Poetry sites on the Internet offer poems you can either choose from and then download or for a fee you can have a poem written specifically for your sweetie. And it's well worth the cost too. (See Fuel Sources at the back of this book.)

♥ Plain old letter paper or notepads with little short love messages you've written. (I love you, hope you have a nice day, thank you for being so wonderful to me, last night was incredible, you are so beautiful. Not so difficult, are they?

♥ Fortune cookies with a fortune written especially for your sweetheart. This company can also be found on the Internet.

♥ Mini-romance novels specifically involving you and your special someone. (See Fuel Sources at the end of this book.)

♥ Love letters of all types. (See Fuel Sources" at the end of this book.)

If harsh words can be referred to as daggers, imagine the goodness kind loving words must create and the positive effects they can have on the people who receive them. There is one important fact you must not forget. No matter how much you lavish your honey with lovely written words, your actions must go along with your prose or it will be meaningless to her.

Cooking is another popular area where a lot of men often find themselves ignorant and therefore cannot perform. How can I describe without going into too much provocative detail the rewards a man can experience by simply knowing how to steam some asparagus? This is definitely when I consider ignorance not being bliss. For those of you who do wish to learn how to cook or already know how, I salute you. These days you can easily learn how to cook gourmet meals, comfort food, and everything in between by simply changing your television from the sports or news channel, once in a while, over to your local food channel. You can also download recipes from the food channel's own website if you are online. They even have short video clips at the website to help you further along.

But if you really want to advance quickly, the next time you visit your local (buy everything in bulk) warehouse, pick up some blank videotapes or DVDs and record your favorite cooking shows. Through television, you can learn how to cook from some of the greatest chefs in the world—right in your own kitchen. Trust me, when you combine the easy-to-follow recipes with the pause and rewind buttons on your recorder's remote, soon you'll be on your way to culinary greatness.

The rewards for being the Wolfgang wannabe in your home can be rather sweet, because most women are crazy about men who can cook.

If you're one of those types who refuses to cook because you're "old-fashioned" or "macho," you're on your own. I'd be surprised to see you got this far into the book. But for all those whose motor skills are no better than those of a toddler or if your work schedule doesn't allow you enough time for cooking, I would like to offer you some solutions to your difficulties. You see, the real beauty of food is that aside from it keeping us alive, there are so many different varieties for us to enjoy. So much of the food we have to choose from doesn't even need to be cooked—only prepared. If you can bathe yourself, shave your face, tie your shoes, or barbeque (barbequing is cooking by the way, but we don't want her to know that) you can prepare meals. I say "prepare" because there is a huge difference between cooking meals and preparing them.

If a man can prepare a golf bag at 5:00 A.M., shoot 18 holes of golf, and calculate his score 14 beers later, he certainly has the intellectual ability to tee up a nice chicken salad for the little lady—and without cooking. At your local grocery market you can find a variety of foods (like ready to eat chicken breast) that have been freshly prepared, precooked, seasoned, sliced, and packaged, all for your convenience. Everything from sliced teriyaki chicken breast to crab salads are at your disposal—ready to plate up and eat.

Gentlemen, ladies are so much easier to please when it comes to food. At least that's been my experience or maybe women's taste buds are programed to enjoy anything prepared by a man for their dining pleasure. Regardless, you don't have to wonder if your honey likes what you plan to prepare for her. Why? Because you—the culinary Casanova—have a list of all her favorite foods in your workbook, many of which can be prepared without ever using a stove top, microwave, or oven.

Here are just a few examples of the type of meals you can prepare for your sweetheart and the kids, without ever cooking. For more no-cook ideas and full recipes free for your consumption, go to http://www.startherheart.com/m_fasttrack.php?Cat_rp=7&es=6. Please note that toasting bread could be considered cooking. But you might want to think twice before telling anybody you don't know how to use a toaster.

No-Cook Food Menu and Meal Ideas

Breakfasts served with coffee, juice or her favorite beverage

♥ Toasted bagels topped with sliced fruit, cinnamon, and honey.

♥ Regular toast, topped with sliced fruit, cinnamon, and honey.

♥ Toasted bagels, topped with plain or flavored cream cheese or jams, and if preferred, gravlax.

♥ Toasted bagels, topped with peanut butter and apples lightly drizzled with honey and sprinkled with cinnamon.

♥ Yogurt, topped with fresh fruit of any kind plus granola cereal.

♥ Store-bought muffins, pastries, scones, or coffee cake.

♥ Cold cereal with fruit and toast, English muffins, or crumpets.

♥ Bowl of freshly chopped fruit salad and toast. Try tossing her fruit salad with a splash of fresh heavy cream, the juice of an orange, lemon, or lime, whichever she prefers, and a light sprinkle of a powdered chile seasoning called "Pico de Gallo," found in the produce department at most grocery markets.

♥ Breakfast bars (granola, protein, or whole grain).

♥ Meal replacement protein shakes. Use soy protein powder if your significant other is experiencing symptoms of beginning her menopause or has already begun. Soy has been proven to naturally increase the estrogen levels in women and helps to dramatically reduce hot flashes—and you will be her hero! Soy is also a good source of protein and may help reduce the risk of heart disease and osteoporosis.

Lunch *or* Dinner

♥ Sandwiches, using any type of bread (bagel, whole wheat, pita bread, or rye—check your list to see what kind of bread is her favorite). Use any fresh deli meats and cheeses (turkey with Swiss cheese, ham with cheddar cheese, the possibilities are almost endless. Don't forget the veggies, lettuce, tomatoes, pickles, on-ions, jalapenos. You can also make her sandwich vegetarian if she prefers it that way.

♥ Fresh fruit served with yogurt.

♥ Salads of any type, chicken (store-bought and precooked), smoked salmon, imitation crab or lump crab meat in the can, or just plain vegetables.

♥ Precooked meats(e.g., rotisserie chicken, barbeque ribs).

♥ Cheese, fruit, crackers, and deli meat platters.

♥ Fresh vegetable with dips.

♥ Chips and salsa with guacamole.

♥ Any restaurants take-out food, plated up nicely at home.

Desserts

♥ Ice creams and sorbet.

♥ Frozen yogurt.

♥ Pie.

♥ Cake.

♥ Cookies.

♥ Anything chocolate.

♥ Fresh fruit with chocolate or other flavored syrup.

♥ Pudding.

♥ Store-bought cheesecake.

♥ Dessert wines, liqueurs, and ports.

You can find numerous assortments of flavors and brands for the food items I just shared with you. There are unlimited combinations in which you can mix and match the preparation of these foods to create continuous variety. Whenever possible try to wow your part-ner by presenting the plate of food with a stylish flare. Your meals will have an even greater impact on her if you let your imagination run wild with your presentations.

My wife goes to pieces when I present most of my dishes. I highly recommend you visit your local mall or Wal-Mart, and find a kitchen utensil store or section. Buy some different-shaped cookie cutters such as hearts, stars, the letters "I" and "U," and whatever you know that she likes. Use the cutters for fruits, cold cuts, cheeses, and finger sandwiches. Be creative and have fun. Surely you'll no longer wait to be fed when you have developed skills to feed others—and not only with food, but with your undeniable will to please and nurture the woman you love and your children.

Now you know how and why you can offer more to the woman in your life. So it's time for you to get behind the wheel and learn exactly what you can give that will positively drive her and keep her driven.

"When a man stops giving he will stop loving and living life as it was meant to be enjoyed."

—Steven A. Guerrero

Good luck with your new adventure. Thank you for reading and don't forget to visit my website at www.StartHerHeart.com for *free* unlimited resources, tips, ideas, and ongoing relationship research.

Congratulations. Now with your sweetheart you can begin to fill in the workbook. By applying what you have already read and using the information in your workbook, there is only one thing left for me to say to you: Gentlemen, start her engine—and keep it running.

"The line between chivalry and chauvinism is a fine one indeed, drawn by man and erased by me."

—Steven A. Guerrero

HER FUEL TANK:
350 Ways to Forever Supercharge Your Lady's Heart

CHAPTER 13

LOCATE HER ENGINE STYLE

Seven Critical Questions

Check the box below that applies to your woman's engine style. If and when you need to refresh your memory of the uniqueness of her engine style you can always refer to the appropriate chapter in Part I of the book.

> ❏ *Diesel engine*—the working woman without children or whose children have grown and gone
>
> ❏ *Economy engine*—the working woman with children or the full-time homemaker with children
>
> ❏ *High-performance engine*—the full-time homemaker without children or whose children have grown and gone

Before you and your darling begin filling out the lists in the workbook, she must answer the following seven critical questions. In questions# 2, 3, 4, and 5 the word "work" relates to anything that is not considered leisure time—cooking, cleaning, doing dishes, grocery shopping, tending to or helping children, maintaining pets, paying bills, doing laundry, ironing, and so forth. You get the idea. And don't you worry, you'll also get a chance to answer the same seven questions although maybe that's not exactly what you where hoping to hear).

Seven Critical Questions

1. What type of job or profession does she have? (full-time home-maker counts as a job)

   _____

2. How many days a week does she work?

   _____

3. How many hours a day does she work?

   _____

4. What time does she have to wake up to get ready for work or help others get ready?

   _____

5. What time does she return home from work or stop working at home?

   _____

6. How much time does she get at the end of each day for relaxing and doing absolutely nothing but resting?

   _____

7. How many children are you raising together and what are their ages?

   _____

Her answers to the seven critical questions can help you see the reality of how busy she really is every day. Hopefully it will help you to understand why she needs your help and appreciation so much. The questions will also help you determine the areas where your help will benefit her the most.

Now it's your turn, gentlemen. Answer the same seven questions. However, answer the questions about yourself.

1. What type of job or profession do you have? (full-time homemaker counts for men too)

   _____

2. How many days a week do you work?

   _____

3. How many hours a day do you work?

   _____

4. What time do you have to wake up to get ready for work or help others get ready?

   _____

5. What time do you return home from work or stop working at home?

   _____

6. How much time do you get at the end of each day for relaxing and doing absolutely nothing but resting?

   _____

7. How many children are you raising together and what are their ages?

   _____

Your own answers can help determine the reasons "why" you can try to improve (not make 50/50) the balance and distribution of the household duties, taking care of the kids, looking after yourself, and taking care of your woman. The load of responsibilities in any household and marriage will never be 50/50. For those who try to keep the score even, raising a big stink when it's 47 to 53 is often the result. For that reason alone, all hell seems to be breaking loose in the scorekeepers' homes. Whatever you do, don't be that way—it's not healthy for anyone or any relationship.

But if the score is obviously unfair, that's not healthy either. Something should be done to correct the matter. If your sweetheart or you feel and maybe even look a little worn-out due to domestic duty disadvantage (DDD), the previous questions can help you understand why. Compare your answers with your honey's answers and it can help the two of you figure out where adjustments can be made and by whom.

In truth, once you've completed this little exercise, it will be plain to see why one of you gets to spend much more time with Homer and Bart. There are almost always adjustments that can be made. Some changes are simple and others can be difficult. It really depends on how far you're willing to go to make your woman happy, without losing yourself.

CHAPTER 14

THE ROMANTIC HISTORY LIST

Special places, events, and dates from your dating years

💜 What is the date you and she first met?	
💜 Where did you and she first meet?	
💜 Where did the two of you go on your first date?	
💜 When and where did the two of you kiss for the first time?	
💜 What is the date you proposed to her?	

♥ Where did you propose to her?	
♥ How did you propose to her?	
♥ Did you have a favorite love song(s) when you were dating? If so, what is the name of the song and artist?	
♥ What was your favorite place to hang out when you were dating?	
♥ What's the date of your wedding anniversary?	
♥ What's the name of the place or church where you got married?	
♥ Where was your wedding reception?	
♥ What is your wedding song(s)?	

♥ Where did you stay on your wedding night?	
♥ What was the suite number where you stayed on your wedding night?	
♥ Where did you go on your honeymoon?	
♥ Where did you stay on your honeymoon?	
♥ What was the number of the honeymoon suite you stayed in on your honeymoon vacation?	
♥ When is her birthday?	

All of the information in your romantic history list can be used anytime to create special themes at home, on weekend getaway trips, or long vacations. It can also help you create custom gifts and keepsakes to give her. But you'll especially benefit by using your romantic history information on those "Special Occasions" such as, birthdays, Christmas, anniversaries, Valentine's Day, Mother's Day, and retirements. However, because you do not want your romantic history to begin seeming as though it is no longer history, I recommend you use this information sparingly.

Unfortunately, everything has the potential to lose its potency. The absence of these particular kinds of nostalgic memories can help the heart continue to grow fond of them. And if you use your romantic history wisely, similar to the example scenarios in the book, the joy you and your special someone experience can last for many years. At least until your marriage is ready for another intoxicating jolt of your romantic history.

CHAPTER 15

THE OLD YOU LIST

These are the things great and small you did in the beginning that caused her to fall in love with you. But now you no longer do them for her. She wishes you would begin to do them again and never stop.

In this list, your honey will tell you exactly what you did in the past that has since vanished from the relationship. Give her some time to think and write down everything she tells you. If you prefer, she can fill this section out herself. Then try your best to be the same man you were when she first fell in love with you. I think you'll be surprised when you see how simple most of the things she mentions will be for you to do again and again and again.

_____

_____

_____

_____

_____

_____

CHAPTER 16

HER FAVORITES LIST

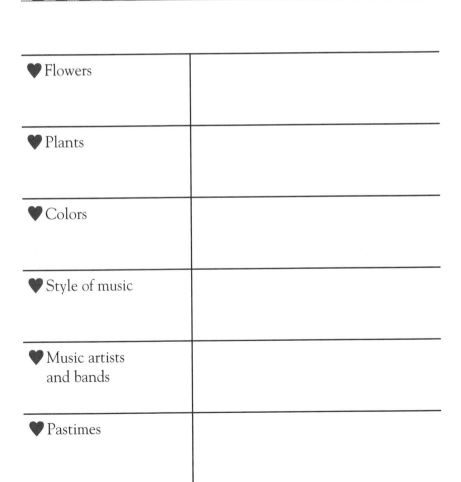

♥ Flowers	
♥ Plants	
♥ Colors	
♥ Style of music	
♥ Music artists and bands	
♥ Pastimes	

♥ Hobbies	
♥ Room in your home	
♥ Ways to relax	
♥ Ambiance	
♥ Home decor style	
♥ Things to do while at home	
♥ Collectable items	
♥ Cartoon characters	
♥ Books, magazines, news-papers and/or sections of, and reading categories	
♥ Authors	

♥ Movie categories (comedy, drama, horror)	
♥ Favorite movie(s)	
♥ Actresses and actors	
♥ Television shows	
♥ Operas	
♥ Comedians	
♥ Painting artists	
♥ Artists in general— and of any type	
♥ Poets and poems	
♥ Pastors, preachers, etc.	

♥ Motivational speakers

♥ Plays

♥ Sports to watch, teams, and players (or drivers)

♥ Sports to play

♥ Method of exercising

♥ Favorite wild animal

♥ Favorite pets

Favorite Food and Beverage Categories

♥ Fruits

♥ Vegetables

♥ Meats

♥ Fish

♥ Ethnic cuisines

♥ Breads

♥ Cheeses

♥ Wines and brands
   of wines

♥ Mixed drinks (liquor
   and brands)

♥ Beers and brands
   of beers

♥ Sodas and brands
   of soda

♥ Waters and brands
   of water

♥ Tea, flavors, brand, creamers, sweeteners	
♥ Coffee, flavor, brands, creamers, sweeteners	
♥ Flavor of milkshake and from where	
♥ Breakfast meals	
♥ Cereals and brands	
♥ Jams or jellies and brands	
♥ Candies	
♥ Ice creams flavors and brands	
♥ Frozen yogurt flavors and brands	
♥ Sorbet flavors and brands	

♥ Cakes and pastries

♥ Pies and other desserts

♥ Chips and brands

♥ Nuts and brands

♥ Condiments and brands

♥ Fresh chilies, or hot sauce or salsa and brands

♥ Spices

♥ Herbs

♥ Dinner appetizers

♥ Oils—olive, sesame, etc.

♥ Milk type and brand	
♥ Overall food to snack on and brand	
♥ Breath mints and brand	
♥ Chewing gum and brand	
♥ Chocolate type— dark, milk, white, etc., and the brand	

Favorite Places

♥ Restaurants, bars, music bars, dance clubs, or hangouts	
♥ Malls	
♥ Stores in the mall	
♥ Clothing stores	

♥ Lingerie stores

♥ Movie theaters

♥ Playhouses

♥ Concert halls, venues, sports stadiums

♥ Beaches

♥ Mountains

♥ Parks

♥ Lakes

♥ Rivers

♥ Countries

♥ States	
♥ Weekend getaway spots	
♥ Longer vacation spots	
♥ Cities	
♥ Hotels	
♥ Bed and breakfasts, inns, lodges	
♥ Resorts	
♥ Health and beauty spas	
♥ Casinos and casino games	
♥ Hair and beauty salons	

♥ Manicurists and nail salons	
♥ Tanning salons	
♥ Churches	
♥ Charities or fund-raising organizations	

Favorite Clothing, Accessories, and Beauty Aids

♥ Her height, weight, bust size, dress size, waist size, pants length, and shoe size	
♥ Clothing designers	
♥ Shoe designers (casual and dressy)	
♥ Athletic shoe brands	
♥ Bra and panties designers	

♥ Hosiery brands or designers and size	
♥ Purse and handbag designers	
♥ Wallet designers	
♥ Belt designers	
♥ Hat designers	
♥ Clothing styles	
♥ Clothing patterns	
♥ Clothing colors	
♥ Shoe colors	
♥ Business suite designers	

♥ Type of jeans and designers	
♥ Coat and jacket designers	

Intimate, Affectionate, and Sexual Favorites

♥ Displays of physical and verbal affections throughout the day and in bed she likes to receive from you— every day	
♥ Methods of foreplay	
♥ Sentimental things you can say and do to make her feel loved, cherished, and appreciated	
♥ Atmosphere or ambiance that gets her in the mood	
♥ Romantic music and artists	
♥ Time of day to make love	

♥ Rooms to make love in	
♥ Places to make love (bed, shower, Jacuzzi, under the stars, etc.)	
♥ Positions to make love	
♥ Words to hear him say to her when they are making love	
♥ Love-making fantasies	
♥ Pet names (honey, babe, sweetheart, etc.)	
♥ Sexual position to climax	
♥ Technique to make her climax	
♥ Bodily area to be touched	
♥ Bodily area to be kissed	

♥ Bodily area to be massaged	
♥ Type of kissing she enjoys	
♥ Gentleman-like qualities and gestures	
♥ Perfumes she likes to wear	
♥ Colognes for you to wear	
♥ Scented candles	
♥ Body and facial washes or soaps	
♥ Shampoos and conditioners	
♥ Body creams	
♥ Facial creams	

♥ Body sprays

♥ Body oils

♥ Massage oils

♥ Powders

♥ Bubble bath products

♥ Bathing and
   mineral salts

Favorite Jewelry

♥ Precious stones

♥ Cuts or shapes of
   precious stones

♥ Precious metals

150

♥ Type of gold

♥ Birthstone

♥ Costume jewelry
designers

♥ Pearls

♥ Type of jewelry (pins,
earrings, finger rings,
toe rings, necklaces,
bracelets, anklets,
body jewelry)

♥ Watch manufactures
and designers

Favorite Things About Him

♥ Way for you to dress

♥ Casual clothing

♥ Dressy clothing

151

♥ Color clothing to see you wear	
♥ Underwear styles	
♥ Shirt styles	
♥ Pants styles	
♥ Shorts styles	
♥ Shoe styles	
♥ Suit styles	
♥ Swimwear styles	
♥ Cologne	
♥ Hair style (if applicable)	

♥ Facial hair style (beard, mustache, etc.)	
♥ Things you says to her	
♥ Things you already do for her	
♥ Memory(ies) of you	
♥ Times to share with you	
♥ Places to be with you	
♥ Things she has done with you	
♥ Trips she has taken with you	
♥ Things she does for you	
♥ Romantic music or love songs you enjoy to listen to together	

Her favorites list will come in handy anytime you're doing something nice for her. It won't matter how often or when you use the information from her favorites list. Unlike the romantic history list, you cannot overuse her favorites list—even if you try. Some of her favorite things can and will change. So don't eliminate the possibility of entering new information once in a while.

I left you plenty of room in the lists to make changes if needed. From her favorites list you'll be able to always incorporate a little something you know she loves into everything you do for her. It is a magical list, however, only when it is used. The more this list is used, the more magical it is.

CHAPTER 17

NOT HER FAVORITES LIST

With your honey go through the "not her favorites" list. Check one of the two boxes provided. For the listed items she doesn't mind doing, enjoys doing, or has plenty of time to get them done, check box "A."

For the items she detests doing, doesn't have time to get to, or really needs your help doing, check box "B."

It's that simple. Don't question her answers. Just finish the list and then you can decide how much of a hero you can and want to be. When a man initiates acts of love, kindness, and consideration, his mate will respond to him in similar ways. The items in this list are things in life and marriage that tend to be underestimated as ways for a man to express his love for a woman. One last thing: If you can afford to hire a household cleaning service and gardener to help ease her load and yours as well, I highly recommend you do.

Box "A" She likes to do, doesn't mind doing or has plenty of time to get done.

Box "B" She detests doing, doesn't have the time to get to, or really needs your help with doing.

A ☺	Cooking and Food Related Category	B ☹
	Breakfast	
	Preparing lunch or making sack lunches	
	Dinner	
	Grocery shopping	
	Making a grocery shopping list	
	Clipping coupons	
	Putting groceries away	
	Carrying in the groceries	
	Taking the children to the market	
A ☺	Cleaning Category	B ☹
	Toilets	
	Bathtubs	
	Showers	
	Sinks	
	Floors	
	Mirrors	
	Faucets	
	Bathrooms entirely	
	Kitchen entirely	

A ☺	Cleaning Category (continued)	B ☹
	Loading and unloading dishwasher	
	Food pantry	
	Refrigerator	
	Freezer	
	Stove	
	Oven	
	Drawers	
	Cupboards	
	Microwave	
	Mopping	
	Dusting	
	Vacuuming	
	Windows	
	Countertops	
	Tile grout	
	Light fixtures	
	Doing dishes	
	Doing laundry	
	Folding the laundry	
	Ironing	

A ☺	**Cleaning Category** (continued)	B ☹
	Going to the dry cleaners	
	Going to the laundromat	
	Making the bed	
	Washing the cars	
	Doing the yard work	
	The garage	
	Cleaning the barbeque	
	Patio	
	Home office	
	Litter boxes	
	Dog, cat, or other pet cleanup	
	Pet cages	
A ☺	**Infant Care**	B ☹
	Feedings, morning, noon, or 3 A.M.	
	Making baby formula	
	Making homemade baby food	
	Bathing	
	Changing diapers	
	Babysitting	

A ☺	Infant Care (continued)	B ☹
	Entertaining the baby	
	Reading to the baby	
	Taking the baby for walks	
	Pushing a stroller	
	Carrying the baby	
	Putting the baby to sleep	
	Doctor visits	
	Shopping for baby items	
	Dropping off baby at the sitter or daycare	
	Picking up baby from the sitter or daycare	
	Getting up at night when baby is sick or hungry	

A ☺	Children	B ☹
	Dropping off at school	
	Picking up from school	
	Helping with homework	
	Helping with school projects	
	Helping with school activities	
	Taking to any after school practices or lessons	
	Enforcing disciplinary actions	

159

A ☺	**Children** (continued)	B ☹
	Talking to them	
	Spending quality time with them—playing together	
	Reading to them	
	Letting them read to you	
	Tucking them into bed	
	Preparing breakfast for them	
	Preparing lunch for them—at home or sack	
	Preparing dinner for them	
	Delegating the chores	
	Seeing that the chores are getting done	
A ☺	**Household and Financial Matters**	B ☹
	Returning video rentals	
	Shopping for the best deal on major purchases	
	Looking for medical doctors	
	Getting an attorney	
	Finding a real estate agent	
	Shopping for a new home	
	Shopping for mortgage rates	
	Shopping for a new car	

A ☺	Household and Financial Matters (continued)	B ☹
	Shopping for insurance	
	Interior mechanical maintenance	
	Exterior mechanical maintenance	
	Automobile maintenance	
	Putting up Christmas lights	
	Taking down Christmas lights	
	Interior holiday decorating	
	Putting away holiday decorations	
	Gift wrapping at Christmas time	
	Shopping for Christmas gifts	
	Shopping for birthday gifts	
	Holiday party planning	
	Trip and vacation planning	
	Arranging social events	
	Planning family events	
	Planing dinner parties at home	
	Paying the bills	
	Balancing the checkbook	
	Creating and monitoring a family budget	
	Preparing the yearly taxes	

A ☺	**Household and Financial Matters** (continued)	B ☹
	Keeping financial records	
	Arranging and keeping track of retirement accounts	
	Shopping for other investments	

CHAPTER 18

HER PET PEEVES AND HURTFUL HABITS LIST

This list speaks for itself. If you want to see a positive change in her—and quickly—just eliminate doing as many things as you can from this list.

♥ The things you say
  that hurt her feelings

♥ The things you do
   that hurt her feelings

♥ The things you don't
   say that hurt her
   feelings

♥ The things you don't
do that hurt her
feelings

♥ Bad habits of yours
that bother her and
she wishes you would
stop doing

♥ Ways in which she feels you take her for granted

♥ Ways in which she feels you take advantage of her

♥ Ways in which she
feels you neglect her

♥ Ways in which she
feels you don't in-
clude her

♥ Ways in which she
feels unappreciated
by you

CHAPTER 19

HER WISH LIST

If she could have the things that are most important to her, provided by you, it would be a wish come true. But for how many people in the world, do their wishes come true, overnight? Not many. And for two people in love, their wish is usually to be able to stay happily together for a lifetime. That is a wish that is still failing to come true for more than 50 percent of those who make it. However, you can beat the odds if you continue to answer her wishes. One at a time will do because a lifetime of little wishes fulfilled is far better than the greatest, fallen ill.

The way to ask your significant other to complete this wish list, is simply by asking her to answer the questions with only the most important things she needs, desires, or wishes to receive from you in all the categories. Then, from this list, it will be up to you to decide what you are capable of achieving to make as many of her wishes as possible become a reality.

♥ What kind of
things can you do
to better support her
emotionally?

♥ What kind of
things can you do
to better support her
spiritually?

♥ What can you do to
    better fulfill her
    physically and
    sexually?

♥ What more can
    you do to help her
    domestically around
    the house?

♥ What more can you
do to help her with
the children?

♥ In what ways and
when would she like
you to show more
affection toward her?

♥ How and when can
you show and express
more appreciation for
her and in what areas
of her life does she
need it most?

♥ What would she like
for you to do for her
and say to her every
day of your life? (Even
when you're angry.)

♥ Places she would love
for you to take her
someday.

♥ Things she would
eventually like for you
to buy, only if it's
affordable at the time.

♥ Those little inexpen-
sive things she would
love for you to buy
her once in a while.

♥ When is it most
important to her that
you say please and
thank you?

♥ What are her
wishes and goals for
financial success and
retirement?

CHAPTER 20

FUEL SOURCES

When you decide to use any of these fuel sources or any other, to create something special for your lady, make sure you have your workbook handy. You can make your gifts super personalized by referring to the detailed information about your special someone. Subsequently, apply anything you know (the more the better) about her to whatever it is you're buying or doing for her. Use her favorite colors, places, foods, pastimes, ways to relax, music, words, flavors, styles, her apparel size, wishes, needs, and so forth.—anything in the workbook—to show her how well you know her and how much you love her. By having so much information about your honey available to you, you will feel like a pro and romance will be a breeze.

♥ You'll find real soul fuel at **timelessmessage.com.** And one bottle your sweetheart certainly won't mind your hitting. You see, this is a "message in a bottle." You know, like sending an SOS to your girl. In this case SOS stands for Sentiments of Sweetness. You can choose your message from their prewritten message library or create your own. Then select one of the many sensual bottles offered in which to send your message, check out, and you're done. It's quick, it's classy, and it's easy. Everything about this product reeks of romance, quality, and care all the way down to the packaging.

Be sure to check out their reminder service. In three simple steps you can be on your way to rescuing your damsel in distress. If possible, send it to her at work. She'll be the envy of her coworkers and you'll be her swashbuckling hero!

♥ When it comes to restaurants, at **zagat.com** you can be just as schooled about great places to dine as Elmer Dills instead of Elmer Fud—picking another dud. Using the Zagat Survey together with your workbook information about her favorite cuisines, foods, music, and ambiance, you can easily locate restaurants she'll enjoy.

Use the survey to locate everything from restaurants that serve massive piles of good affordable linebacker grub to those joints that charge you a week's salary for two snails, four splinters from a carrot, and a chickpea. The restaurants in the survey are rated on the overall food, decor, service, and cost. It's a giant stress reliever, especially helpful when you're planning a vacation. In any area you'll be visiting, before you even leave your house you can determine where all the good food in your price range is located. Then you can make advance reservations and get directions. Your sweetheart will be impressed by your preparedness.

♥ Take any dinner occasion to the next level and make it a meal to remember for her. Order a poetic dinner menu. Anniversaries, birthdays, Valentine's Day, a marriage proposal, or just because, this menu will nourish her soul for good. Go to **StartHerHeart.com** to find out how you can purchase this supper shocker for your sweetheart.

♥ This is a great reliable source to locate bed and breakfast lodging all over the world. If your sweetheart enjoys the bed and breakfast scene (some people don't, so check your workbook first), then **www.bbchannel.com** is your one-stop shop, especially when you know her favorite cities, states, and countries to visit—or that she wishes to visit eventually.

♥ Wow! So far the folks at **YourNovel.com** have produced 13 custom romance novels. Each of the books can be personalized with you and your sweetheart's information. You might not look like Fabio, but you don't need to because, from mild to wild, in these books you're her hero, so pick a passion and let them work their magic. Try giving your custom novel to her using the bookstore special occasion scenario found on page 102.

♥ Another website where you can create your own personalized romance novel starring you and your sweetheart is at **www.Book ByYou.com**. There are three passionate stories to choose from and the site offers you a free personalized preview of each novel. Just complete the nine one-word questions, then click "view," and you can read three excerpts from the book with you and your honey as the star characters. It's fun and romantic reading.

♥ Some men have difficulty deciding how to surprise their sweetheart, or with what. Well, at **surprise.com** they cure the aforementioned male ailments—or "malements" for short—by offering more gift categories and gift ideas than you can imagine. Next time you want to surprise your honey, spend a few minutes at www. surprise.com and be surprised at how easy it can really be to startle your sweetie.

♥ ***Don't Sweat the Small Stuff in Love*** by Dr. Richard Carlson, Ph.D, is to my book's Chapter 6, "Racing to Win—Don't Crash and Burn" what a fire extinguisher is to a race car driver. Dr. Carlson's book fills people with ways to smother the silly "not worth it" things that anger them and can eventually ruin their relationship, while he directs their focus to the meaningful things that can strengthen their love. Remember that when it comes to relationships, we can't stop the crashes, but we can certainly prevent the burning that destroys them. At **DontSweat.com** you can order the book, and while you're there, take a peek at his whole line of antiperspirants for the armpits of life.

♥ When you've completed Parts I and II of the *Gentlemen, Start Her Engine* book and workbook, author and romance guru Gregory Godek has an awesome book for you: ***1001 Ways to Be Romantic.*** Gregory also has many other great books on romance for you to check out as well—and all of them can be effective for creating and nurturing love and romance within your relationship. You can find Gregory's books at most major bookstores and online at **Amazon.com.**

♥ Everything you'd want to know about food and cooking is at FoodTV.com. They have great recipes from many famous chiefs and you can download any of them. In the recipe and site search box, type in the food you're thinking of preparing. For example, type in chicken and you'll get some 2,805 recipes from greats like Wolfgang Puck, Emeril Lagasse, Bobby Flay, Martha Stewart, and many other top chiefs.

Regardless of your cooking skills the printable recipes, ingredient lists, measurements, and step-by-step instructions practically take you by the hand and transform you into a gourmet cook.

If you want to make things quick and foolproof, simply record your favorite cooking show and play it back when you're ready to start preparing your meal. Another great resource at the site is a show called "Food Finds." Go into "choose a show," click on "food finds," then press go.

You can also order decadent desserts as well as other foods from all over the United States.

♥ If you're afraid of burning the house down, or you're too busy to prepare meals at home, go to **http://www.startherheart.com/ m_fasttrack.php?Cat_rp=7&es=6** and get ideas and recipes for no-cook meals and desserts.

♥ If you and the someone you love have e-mail, this site can keep you in touch with one another in a very touching way. It's the e-cards and flash e-cards that are making the world lovingly go round. E-cards for every occasion you can dream of are free at **123greetings.com;** you can type a short message and send it off to your sweetheart. The e-cards are fully animated and even have music you can choose to go along with your e-mail. Your honey will be e-lated—and you won't be disappointed either—and it's free!

♥ For even more e-cards and greetings to choose from you've got to check out **ecardsaddict.com.** Lots and lots of fun, sexy, romantic stuff at this website. You won't be sorry you visited.

♥ There is a great poetry website at **lovepoemsandquotes.com**— and you'll actually be able to understand the poems. There are many other useful tools of the sentiment trade here, so use them excessively and your relationship will flourish.

♥ Visit **lovestories.com** and you'll have access to nearly 26,000 great poems, 800 or so love stories, 300 plus journals, and almost 200 essays all about love.

♥ When you want to treat your sweetheart to something special, arrange a trip to a travel spa or book her a few hours or an entire day at any of the local day spas to choose from at **SpaFinder.com.** Spa Finder offers you modestly priced spas to choose from but leaves you with plenty of ways to get $oaked if you can afford to or want to. If you're the (handyman) type (lucky her) view the Spa Finder's spa store at the site. There you can save money ordering your own home spa therapy kit.

♥ At **GiftBasketBoutique.com** you can fill her heart as well as her tummy by having your own personal message—up to 10 sentences long—inserted into a giant fortune cookie.

Attention, Gentlemen!

Did any ideas in the *Gentlemen, Start* Her *Engine—and Keep It Running* book/workbook bring good fortune to your relationship? Did this book help you to create new, easy, creative ways to bring joy to the woman you love? If so, then I would like to hear your stories. Feel free to share your successes, tips and ideas with me.

Attention, Ladies!

I invite you to share your stories about the wonderful things your man does to drive you wild, and keep your motor and relationship running strong. All submissions will be entered into a drawing for great prizes monthly. Send yours today for a chance to make your sweetheart the StartHerHeart.com Gentleman of the Month. All stories must indicate the woman's style to be eligible for the monthly drawing.

Send mail to:
Gentlemen, Start *Her* Engine—and Keep It Running
Attn: Readers' Successes and Ideas
324 S. Diamond Bar Blvd., PMB 350
Diamond Bar, CA 91765
Please include your woman's engine style at the top of your letters.

You can also e-mail your stories to me at:
VictoryLane@StartHerHeart.com

All submissions become the property of *Gentlemen, Start* Her *Engine—and Keep It Running* and cannot be returned.

Find a lot more tips and ideas that work
for the style of your woman at:
www.StartHerHeart.com